What Are They Saying About the Formation of Israel?

John J. McDermott

PAULIST PRESS
New York/Mahwah, N.J.

Cover design by James Brisson

Library of Congress Cataloging-in-Publication Data

McDermott, John J.,   1960–
    What are they saying about the formation of Israel? / John J. McDermott.
        p.   cm.
    Includes bibliographical references.
    ISBN 0–8091–3838–7 (alk. paper)
    1. Jews—History—1200–953 B.C.—Historiography. 2. Bible. O.T. Former Prophets—Historiography. 3. Palestine—Ethnology. 4. Canaanites—Historiography. 5. Jews—Origin. I. Title.
DS121.55.M35   1998
930′.04924—dc21   98–43114
                                                                                          CIP

Published by Paulist Press
997 Macarthur Boulevard
Mahwah, New Jersey 07430

www.paulistpress.com

Printed and bound in the
United States of America

Contents

Acknowledgments

There are many people who helped, both directly and indirectly, to make this work possible. I first want to thank my editor at Paulist Press, Fr. Lawrence Boadt, C.S.P., for his encouragement and practical suggestions. Fr. Robert Beck of Loras College read the manuscript and offered several useful suggestions. I also want to express my gratitude to the scripture teachers I have had, who opened up the world of the Bible to me, especially Fr. Harry Hagan, O.S.B., and Fr. Damien Dietlein, O.S.B., at St. Meinrad School of Theology, and Fr. Augustine Gianto, S.J., at the Pontifical Biblical Institute. Finally, this work would not have been possible without the love and support of my parents, Arlene McDermott and the late Edward McDermott, who first inspired in me a love of learning.

1
The Issue

The Pentateuch and the Book of Joshua tell a continuous story of the beginnings of the Israelites. A group of descendants of Abraham escaped from slavery in Egypt under the leadership of Moses. After journeying forty years through the desert, they crossed the Jordan River into the land of Canaan. In a series of battles, these Israelites conquered one Canaanite city after another. Halfway through the Book of Joshua the conquest is declared complete, with the Israelites having successfully taken the entire nation; the book then lists the cities and kings they defeated. The second half of Joshua describes the division of the land among the tribes of the Israelites. The book concludes with all of the Israelites coming together at Shechem for a covenant renewal ceremony.

This biblical story has always been of great interest because of its theological importance. It is the foundational story of Judaism and Christianity. The story of a people's origins expresses their central beliefs about themselves. In recent decades this story has also been one of the most debated issues among archaeologists and historians. Several theories have been proposed in the past to explain Israel's beginnings. Today there is a wealth of new evidence that raises questions about past theories.

It is clear that there are problems with viewing the biblical description of Israel's beginnings as literal history. The first is that there are contradictions between different parts of the Bible. Joshua says the conquest was completely successful:

> So Joshua took all that land: The hill country and all the Negeb and all the land of Goshen and the lowland and the Arabah and the hill country of Israel and its lowland, from Mount Halak, which rises toward Seir, as far as Baal-gad in the valley of Lebanon below Mount Hermon. He took all their kings and struck them down, and put them to death. (Jos 11:16–17)

Chapter 12 of Joshua goes on to list the conquered kings and cities, including the cities of Jerusalem (Jebus), Hebron and Taanach, among others.

The Book of Judges gives a very different picture. It opens with a description of the places not yet conquered by the Israelites. The unconquered territory includes "the Canaanites who lived in the hill country, in the Negeb, and in the lowland" (Jgs 1:9), and the cities of Jebus, Hebron and Taanach; that is, some of the very same places that the Book of Joshua lists as successfully conquered by the Israelites, Judges documents as not yet conquered. Judges as a whole gives the impression of a long, continuing battle between the newly arrived Israelites and the Canaanites, who continued to hold on to much of the territory; and it is not until the beginning of the monarchy, in the Second Book of Samuel, that King David takes the city of Jerusalem from the Canaanites.

Besides the contradictions within different parts of the Bible, there are problems reconciling archaeological data with the stories in the Pentateuch, Joshua and Judges. The stories in Genesis dealing with Abraham, Isaac and Jacob are not the types of stories that are easily verified through archaeological evidence. The people lived in tents and migrated from place to place; most of the recorded incidents involved family sagas rather than major national events that would be memorialized with monuments or buildings. In some cases we can look at the mores of the people in

Genesis and compare them to what is known from other sources of ancient Near Eastern customs. For example, marriage customs, the selling of a birthright and other such traditions have often been compared to parallels in texts from Nuzi, in Mesopotamia, written in the fifteenth and fourteenth centuries B.C.E.[1] But the parallels are not exact and in any case are not conclusive proof that the events are historically accurate.

Moreover, there is good reason to believe that the stories in Genesis were written centuries after they supposedly occurred. There are anachronisms: for instance, Genesis mentions Abraham encountering Philistines (Gn 21:22–34), but archaeological evidence and written sources from Egypt make it clear that the Philistines did not arrive in Canaan until around 1200 or 1150 B.C.E., long after Abraham would have lived. Most biblical scholars believe the Pentateuch was not finished before the fifth century B.C.E., which would explain its anachronisms and raise questions about whether any of it is historically reliable. Most scholars see only fragmentary historical memories in Genesis.[2]

Proving the historicity of the Exodus story is also problematic. The Book of Exodus describes a series of catastrophic events in Egypt (the plagues), ending with the death of all the firstborn of the Egyptians. Some have argued that all of the plagues are similar to natural phenomena in Egypt (e.g., silt occasionally turning the Nile a reddish color) and that something like the parting of the sea could have occurred naturally. If in fact all of these events did take place in the magnitude in which Exodus describes them and all within a short period of time, one would expect it to be recorded in some source other than the Bible. No Egyptian records, however, mention the events of the Exodus.

Similarly, archaeological evidence (discussed in chapter 2) does not support the Book of Joshua's claim of an all-at-once military conquest of Canaan. Several cities that it cites as having been conquered and destroyed by the Israelites show no evidence of destruction. In some instances, such as those of Jericho and Ai, the locations cited were not even inhabited at the time.[3] Additional archaeological evidence gleaned from analyses of the pottery, house types and new settlements also makes it all but certain that the story of a successful conquest of Canaan by a group of Israelites coming in from the outside is not historically accurate.

Scholars recognize that the biblical story of the beginnings of Israel has a theological purpose. It expresses the fulfillment of the promises that God made to the chosen people—Abraham and his descendants. The center of the promise was that God would give them a land of their own. Joshua portrays God as faithfully fulfilling that promise. The stories in the Pentateuch, Joshua and Judges contain various amounts of history and legend, shaped over time to express the theological message clearly. The community's goal in retelling the story was not the preservation of history for its own sake, but rather to teach each new generation the ways of God.

If, then, the biblical account of Israelite origins is not literal history, what is the historical origin of these people? Archaeological discoveries in Palestine and the discoveries of inscriptions and documents from Egypt and elsewhere have added enormously to our knowledge of the ancient Near East, but the evidence is open to various interpretations. Scholars have come up with different answers to the question by putting the pieces together differently.

What is known is that during the Late Bronze Age (ca. 1550–1200 B.C.E.), Egypt ruled over a large empire, including the land that later became Israel. That land was known as Canaan at the time. In Canaan were several large, fortified cities ruled by local kings governing as vassals of Egypt. Although the Egyptian army was strong enough to maintain stability in Canaan, there were threats to that stability. Occasionally Egypt had to put down resistance to its rule; also, the local Canaanite kings were often at battle against each other. Moreover, the powerful Hittite kingdom to the north fought against Egypt for supremacy in the ancient Near East.

In the thirteenth and twelfth centuries B.C.E., the stability provided by Egyptian power came to an end. A major war with the Hittites shortly after 1300 weakened Egypt and ended its hopes of controlling the entire ancient Near East. Eventually Egypt lost control of Canaan. There is evidence of some Canaanite cities being destroyed and of others losing population. There are also indications of new settlements having been made in the poorer hill country of Canaan. There were also migrations of various peoples, including a group called the Philistines, who settled in Canaan.

The years from 1200 to 1000 B.C.E. were a time of transition in Canaan. All of the factors that led to the decline of the previous status quo are not known, but the final outcome is evident. After a period of instability, with various groups struggling for control of the land, a people known as the Israelites emerged as the dominant group. They established a kingdom (later split into two separate kingdoms) that lasted for several centuries. The religious literature of the Israelites became the Hebrew Scriptures, or Old Testament.

Who were these Israelites and where did they come from? The tools that scholars use to answer that question include a critical reading of the biblical and nonbiblical texts, as well as archaeological data and theories from the social sciences. In the past, one type of evidence has been used almost to the exclusion of all others. Before modern archaeological study, the Bible was the only source of information on Israelite history and was usually taken literally. Even those who became convinced that it was not literal history still had to come up with a critical reinterpretation of the Bible itself in order to reconstruct Israelite history.

Today, however, the opposite is often the case for several reasons: (1) there is a wealth of archaeological evidence available; (2) the Old Testament was written centuries after the beginnings of Israel; (3) some of the stories clearly are not historical; and (4) attempts to decide which details are historical and which are not can seem very subjective; some scholars prefer to rely only on archaeology and other evidence outside the Bible to reconstruct early Israelite history. Referring to biblical stories about the origin of the Israelites, T. L. Thompson stated, "…the historical problem is not so much that they are historically unverifiable, and especially not that they are untrue historically, but that they are radically irrelevant as sources of Israel's early history."[4]

In this book I will look at evidence both from the Bible and from outside the Bible because in fact most scholars do use both. Chapter 2 will be a review of the available archaeological data and textual sources outside the Bible. Chapters 3 through 7 will describe how scholars in the past and in the present have used the available data to explain Israel's beginnings. The first step, though, will be a critical look for historical data in the biblical texts that deal with the origin of the Israelites.

The stories of Abraham, Isaac and Jacob in the Book of Genesis do not give us any direct evidence for how the nation of Israel emerged in Canaan around the year 1200 B.C.E. The patriarchal stories are set much earlier and are really stories about a family rather than a nation. However, in an indirect way the patriarchal stories are helpful tools for examining the origins of the Israelite nation. The lifestyles of Abraham, Isaac and Jacob greatly resemble the ways of nomads. They migrated from place to place, occasionally encountering Canaanite or Egyptian rulers, but they did not establish permanent cities of their own. Sometimes they intermarried with the Canaanites (Judah in Gn 38) but, for the most part, did not.

The significance of this description of their lifestyle is disputed. At first glance it would seem to support a theory of nomadic roots for the Israelites. Norman Gottwald, however, says that it could indicate that the Israelites' beginnings were in rural communities based upon diversified agriculture and that they were not necessarily involved in regular nomadism.[5] In any case, the descriptions of the lifestyles of the patriarchs tell us that our search for Israelite origins should include studies of nomadic as well as other peoples in the region.

In the next part of this story, the escape from Egypt, there is a great diversity of opinions. The closest thing to a consensus among scholars is that something similar to the Exodus could have occurred but not in the exact way described in the Book of

Exodus. Several details seem legendary. Could a Hebrew slave girl really walk right up to the daughter of the pharaoh in the palace (Ex 2:1–10)? Could there have been 600,000 men and their families, plus a mixed crowd that went out with them, in a single group journeying through the desert (Ex 12:37–38)? The plagues are also hard to accept as historical. Although it may be true that they are all similar to natural phenomena in Egypt, if all of these plagues had occurred one after another, surely the effect on Egypt would have been disastrous and there would have been some mention of it in some Egyptian source.

John Bright, in his *A History of Israel,* states that there must be some historical basis to the story of the enslavement because it is not the kind of story that people invent for themselves. But he acknowledges that they probably embellished parts of it to make its theological teaching clearer; he also states that the numbers involved had to be much smaller than those that the Bible suggests.[6] Other scholars, such as Baruch Halpern, who see some historical truth in the Exodus story agree that a small group of Semitic slaves escaped from Egypt. Egypt did use Semitic slaves in some state building projects, and occasionally a few slaves escaped. A small group of escaped slaves would not have been considered significant by the Egyptians, and such a band could have made its way to Canaan and become part of the emerging Israelite people.[7] Niels Peter Lemche, however, takes a more skeptical view of the biblical traditions because they were composed so much later than the events they describe and underwent complex redactions through the centuries. In his history of Israel he does not use the Exodus story as a literal source.[8]

The biblical story goes on to relate, in the Book of Joshua, that these people conquered the entire land of Canaan in a series of battles. From the archaeological evidence discussed below, it is unlikely that this claim is historically accurate. It is also clear that the Book of Joshua has a theological purpose. In their commentary on Joshua, Robert Boling and G. Ernest Wright explain that the book portrays God as fulfiller of the promise made to Abraham to give his descendants a land, and as a divine warrior acting on their behalf. When the Israelites follow the laws of the covenant, they are successful in battle. When they disobey, they are defeated in battle (e.g., their first attempt to capture Ai, in Jos 7).[9] The purpose of the Book of Joshua is not to record history, but to say something about God's relationship with the Israelites. It should therefore be used as a historical source only with great caution.

The Book of Judges also describes a series of battles, but again the book clearly has a theological purpose. In Judges the same pattern is repeated several times: the Israelites are unfaithful to the covenant; God allows their enemies to defeat them; they cry out to God for help; God raises up a "judge" who saves the Israelites in battle; the land enjoys peace for a number of years. Like Joshua, the book is not written to record history, but to say something about the Israelites' relationship with God.

Joshua and Judges may not be recorded history, but they should not be dismissed out of hand. There is good evidence that some of the events in the books are based on history; for example, the story of the migration of the tribe of Dan from the coast near the southern tribes to northern Galilee is supported by archaeological evidence (see chapter 4). The very fact that the books use stories of battles to talk about their national origins should lead us to suspect that some battles were involved. Because the land of Canaan was in a time of transition, it is only reasonable to expect some battles between different groups vying for control of territories. The books of Joshua and Judges have taken memories of a few historical battles and settlements and migrations of peoples and made them part of a much more elaborate story of a conquest of all of Canaan.

Although it is impossible to know for certain which details in Joshua and Judges might be historical and which not, one approach is to look at the earliest parts of the books. Presumably, something written closer to the time of the events described would likely be more accurate than parts of the books written centuries later. Based on linguistic analysis and comparison with other ancient Near Eastern poetry, F. M. Cross and D. N. Freedman, in a study of early Hebrew poetry, concluded that Judges 5 is an archaic Hebrew victory song written before 1000 B.C.E.[10] Judges 5 celebrates a victory of the Israelite tribes over Canaanite kings. However, not all of the tribes participated in the battle. In the song, some tribes are praised for joining Ephraim and Manasseh, the central tribes close to the scene of the battle (Benjamin, Zebulun, Issachar and Naphtali). Others are cursed for not joining (Reuben, Gilead, Dan and Asher). Others are not even mentioned (the southern tribes Judah and Simeon).

If the song reflects historical reality, it reveals the lack of unity among the tribes. Sometimes they cooperated with each other in times of battles against a common enemy. Sometimes they failed to help out when they were expected to, and the southern tribes, Judah and Simeon, apparently were not even expected to join the others, as they are neither praised nor cursed. If the southern early Israelites were not united with the north and if those in the north were inconsistent in their unity, perhaps we should not expect a single explanation for the origin of the people who became Israelites. Perhaps they lacked unity in the tribal period because they came from diverse backgrounds before the tribal period.

Another reason many scholars believe parts of Judah had a separate origin from other Israelites is the Caleb tradition in Numbers, Deuteronomy and Joshua. Numbers 13–14 tells of the attempts to spy out the land from the south, for which Caleb is rewarded for his bravery while the rest of the Israelites are criticized for their fear of entering the land. Deuteronomy 1:19–40 summarizes the same story. Joshua 14:6–15 tells of Joshua granting the region of Hebron to Caleb the Kenizzite as a reward for his earlier bravery. The biblical story is thus trying to explain why there is a different group of people from a different background in the land that is part of Judah.[11]

In fact, it was only during a small part of the biblical period that all of the Israelites were politically united. The large kingdom of David and Solomon was the exception, not the rule, although the Hebrew Scriptures see it as the ideal intended by God. If the people who became the Israelites were not united during most of the biblical period, looking for different origins for different segments of the Israelite people might make more sense than looking for one single model that assumes a unity that was not there.

Used critically, the Hebrew Scriptures can suggest some possibilities for the origins of the Israelites. The Bible cannot be used as evidence that all of the Israelites descended from Abraham, Isaac and Jacob and from people who had been slaves in Egypt, nor that the emergence of Israel was mainly a military process. There *may* have been some nomadic people who became part of the Israelites and whose stories became the background for the patriarchal stories. There *may* have been a group of escaped slaves from Egypt who made its way to Canaan and became part of the emerging Israelites. It is likely that the beginnings of Israel involved at least some battles, and there is much evidence in the Bible that we should not look for one origination process for the Israelites, but for a history involving multiple origins.

A critical reading of the biblical texts broadens the horizon for further study. The historical significance of the various "clues" in the Bible provides a basis for different interpretations. Accurate theories about the beginnings of Israel depend on combining the biblical evidence with that gathered from sources outside the Bible.

2
Textual and Archaeological Evidence

Over the last 150 years, our knowledge of the Bible has been greatly enhanced by the discovery of other texts from the ancient Near East and by archaeological discoveries. This chapter will review the written and material remains from Israel and the surrounding regions and will discuss how that data adds to our knowledge of Israel's beginnings. To better organize this large amount of material, I will treat it in two parts—first, texts and, second, other material remains. Obviously the interpretation of the two is related because texts form a part of a people's material culture and because the interpretation of texts often depends on an awareness of the settings in which they were found and of other objects associated with them.

The evidence will not answer every question about the Israelites' origins, but I am especially interested in what it says about two issues. First, did the Israelites come to Canaan from the outside, or were they indigenous to the land? Second, was the emergence of Israel mainly a peaceful process or a violent affair? Theories that have been proposed for the origin of the Israelites differ on these issues, and answers to them will go a long way toward evaluating the theories.

In the discussion that follows I will refer to the time periods in which these events took place, using standard archaeological terms. It is necessary to be aware of the following periods:

Late Bronze Age	1550–1200 B.C.E.
Iron Age I	1200–1000 B.C.E.
Iron Age II	1000–586 B.C.E.

These terms can be misleading; the use of *bronze* or *iron* is not actually the most important characteristic of these periods; during the early part of the Iron Age, bronze was still used more than iron, and the changes from one period to the next were gradual, so there is a great deal of overlap in the characteristics of the periods.

Part I: Texts

Textual evidence includes any written source from Egypt, Canaan or the surrounding regions, dating from around the time that Israel began, that might in any way tell us something of its beginnings. The textual evidence, of course, has to be used in a critical way. Just as the Bible's main purpose is not the recording of history, so too nonbiblical written remains may focus on various civilizational aspects of a culture other than the accurate reporting of history, thus exaggerating or revising historical events in the same way the Bible does.

A. The Amarna Letters

The most useful textual source from Egypt is a collection of writings called the Amarna letters. Discovered in 1887 at Tell el-Amarna in Egypt, the letters were written from Canaanite cities under Egyptian rule during the fourteenth century B.C.E. They give us a picture of Canaan when it was ruled through a system of city-states. The kings of Canaanite cities had a large amount of local control but were still vassals of Egypt and were dependent on the Egyptian army for security. Many of the letters are complaints from one local king that a neighboring king is encroaching on his territory and that therefore the Egyptians should send their chariots in to set things right. The letters most relevant to a biblical study can be found in James Pritchard's collection, *Ancient Near Eastern Texts Relating to the Old Testament;*[1] a complete collection is William Moran's *The Amarna Letters.*[2]

The Amarna letters mention a group called the *hapiru* (also spelled *apiru* or *habiru* by some). The Canaanite kings complain of raids by the *hapiru* on their fields and villages. They also complain that other kings hire the *hapiru* as mercenaries. The *hapiru* do not seem to be a separate ethnic group, but rather a social class of dispossessed people. They were not residents of the cities, but rather lived in gangs in the countryside. One letter refers to some of them as former slaves.[3] Although most of the letters express fear or annoyance regarding the *hapiru,* one letter reveals a sympathetic attitude toward them.[4] A common fear often expressed in the letters is that people will kill their leaders and join the *hapiru* and that more and more land will come under *hapiru* control. One characteristic letter reads in part:

> To Amanappa, my father: Message of Rib-Hadda, your son....If this year no archers come out, then all the lands will be joined to the Apiru. If the king, my lord, is negligent and there are no archers, then let a ship fetch the men of Gubla, your men and the gods to bring them all the way to you so I can abandon Gubla. Look, I am afraid the peasantry will strike me down.[5]

The significance of this information on the *hapiru* is that it gives us a fuller picture of the population of Canaan. Some have suggested that they were the ancestors of the Hebrews. The names *hapiru* and *Hebrew* may be etymologically related: the *hapiru* were people of a lower-class background, and their history of conflict with Canaanite cities corresponds roughly to the picture that we get from the books of Joshua and Judges. George Mendenhall and Norman Gottwald have made much of a possible *hapiru* role in the formation of the Israelites, suggesting that they were instrumental in stirring up other dispossessed people to revolt against the ruling kings.[6] The letters that refer to people killing their leaders and joining the *hapiru* and to land coming under *hapiru* control could fit the Canaanite view of a social revolution. While others disagree on how significant the *hapiru* were, their presence must be kept in mind in considering the situation out of which Israel emerged.

B. Egyptian Encounters with the Shasu

Besides the Amarna letters, there are numerous records of military campaigns of the Egyptian kings in Canaan and elsewhere, celebrating their success in keeping order in their territories. A group of people mentioned occasionally in these military encounters from about 1500 to 1150 B.C.E. is the *shasu*.[7] The *shasu* were a nomadic people who took their flocks from place to place and often disturbed the Egyptians, who didn't like the idea of random groups coming and going as they pleased through their kingdom. Various Egyptian records mention battles in which the *shasu* were either driven out of Egypt or captured as slaves. Other records mention peaceful arrangements whereby the *shasu* were allowed to pass through for the payment of a tax.[8]

The *shasu* are also tempting designates for the ancestors of the Israelites. Their nomadic lifestyle and their encounters with the Egyptians conform closely to the picture that we get in the Book of Genesis sagas of Abraham, Isaac and Jacob. Some historians, such as Donald Redford in *Egypt, Canaan and Israel in Ancient Times,* see the *shasu* as people who gradually settled down in villages in Canaan, eventually becoming integrated with the Israelites.[9] Redford and others have also claimed that there is evidence of *shasu* who worshiped Yahweh before the beginnings of Israel. In a list of *shasu* locations, one name mentioned is "Yhw in the land of the *shasu*," possibly referring to a group of *shasu* who named their enclave after the god they worshiped—

Yahweh.[10] Others disagree with that conclusion, including Gösta Ahlström and Thomas Thompson,[11] but if it is true, then there is even more reason for thinking that some of the *shasu* could have become Israelites. Of course, if some *shasu* became Israelites, that does not mean that all or even the majority of Israelites had been *shasu*.

C. Egyptian Encounters with the Sea Peoples

Another group of people Egyptian records mention near the beginning of Iron Age I are the Sea Peoples. *Sea Peoples* is a collective term for groups who migrated from the region of the Aegean Sea to other places in the eastern Mediterranean, including Egypt and Canaan, during the thirteenth and twelfth centuries B.C.E. For students of the Bible, the best known of these people are the Philistines, who constituted only one group among these migrants; others included the Tjeker, Shekelesh, Denyen and Weshesh.

The Philistines and other Sea Peoples have been studied extensively by Trude and Moshe Dothan, who have done much to dispel the notion that the Philistines were barbaric people of no culture compared to the Israelites. In *The Philistines and Their Material Culture*[12] and *People of the Sea: The Search for the Philistines,*[13] they have revealed the well-developed culture and complex history of the Philistines.

An important inscription mentioning several Sea Peoples was discovered at Medinet Habu, a mortuary temple of Rameses III in Egypt, dating from the early twelfth century B.C.E. In the inscription, Rameses III celebrates his victory over people who have invaded from the sea.

> Their confederation was the Philistines, Tjeker, Shekelesh, Denyen, and Weshesh, lands united. They laid their hands upon the lands as far as the circuit of the earth, their hearts confident and trusting: "Our plans will succeed!"...Those who reached my frontier, their seed is not, their heart and

> their soul are finished forever and ever....They are capsized
> and overwhelmed where they are. Their heart is taken away,
> their soul is flown away. Their weapons are scattered upon
> the sea.[14]

On the walls of Medinet Habu are reliefs depicting battles both on land and at sea. Besides warriors, the reliefs show oxcarts with women and children, providing evidence that the Sea Peoples were not just invading armies, but were whole communities searching for new land in which to settle.[15]

Another text from the twelfth century B.C.E. also mentions Rameses III's dealings with the Sea Peoples.

> I slew the Denyen in their islands, while the Tjeker and the
> Philistines were made ashes. The Sherden and the Weshesh
> of the sea were made nonexistent, captured all together and
> brought in captivity to Egypt like the sands of the shore. I set-
> tled them in strongholds, bound in my name. Their military
> classes were numerous as hundred-thousands. I assigned
> portions for them all with clothing and provisions from the
> treasuries and the granaries every year.[16]

This passage gives an explanation for how the Philistines and other Sea Peoples came to be living in Canaan, Egyptian-controlled territory, despite Rameses III's claim that he repelled them from his lands. They were hired as mercenaries and assigned to fortresses in Canaan. Actually because Egyptian power would shortly decline, other Sea Peoples besides the ones hired as mercenaries were probably able to settle in Canaan on their own.

In the Bible the Philistines became the major enemy of the Israelites and are portrayed as people completely distinct from the Israelites. But it is necessary to look at the arrival of the Philistines in studying the origin of the Israelites because they arrived around the same time as Israel's beginnings and may have affected events. Also, if it is true that the Israelites were a people of mixed background, it is possible that some of the Sea Peoples became part of the Israelites.

D. The Merneptah Stele

One other Egyptian written source relevant to the beginning of Israel is the Merneptah Stele.[17] Merneptah was king of Egypt late in the thirteenth B.C.E. century. The Merneptah Stele is a monument that he erected to celebrate his victories (certainly exaggerated) over those who resisted his rule. Near the end of the text, the name *Israel* occurs in a list of places and peoples in Canaan defeated by Merneptah.

> The princes are prostrate, saying: Mercy!
> Not one raises his head among the Nine Bows.
> Desolation is for Tehenu; Hatti is pacified;
> Plundered is the Canaan with every evil;
> Carried off is Ashkelon; seized upon is Gezer;
> Yanoam is made as that which does not exist;
> Israel is laid waste, his seed is not;
> Hurru is become a widow for Egypt!
> All lands together, they are pacified;
> Everyone who was restless, he has been bound.[18]

Of interest is the way the name *Israel* is written. Hasel and others who have studied the inscription point out that instead of being written with the sign for a nation or city, Israel is written with the sign for a people, possibly indicating a tribal or nomadic group with that name.[19]

The Merneptah Stele is the earliest written reference to Israel. It tells us that around the year 1200 B.C.E., there was an identifiable group of people collectively called Israel somewhere in the land of Canaan. As a name on a list, the reference doesn't tell us very much. It does not tell us how large this Israel was, how long the group had been in existence, or exactly where the Israelites lived. It does, however, provide evidence for their existence and shows that they were a people who resisted Egyptian rule.

Frank Yurco has suggested that a relief discovered at the temple of Karnak in Egypt depicts the same military campaign referred to on the Merneptah Stele.[20] Although others, including Anson Rainey, have disputed the claim,[21] Yurco's suggestion, if correct, can be interpreted as showing the Israelites dressed the same as other Canaanites and not like the nomadic *shasu,* indicating the early Israelites were indigenous to Canaan and not people who had migrated there from the desert.

Summary of Egyptian Sources

The Egyptian sources supply us with a great deal of information. They paint a picture of a Canaan ruled through a system of city-states just before Israel emerged. They tell us that Egypt was trying to hold on to its rule through military campaigns. They give us information on several different groups of people living in and around Canaan, including one called Israel. From the Egyptian sources we know much about the setting out of which Israel was formed, but we still do not know the specific facts of how it actually emerged.

E. Ugaritic Texts and Other Sources on Canaanite Religion

In 1928 some ancient ruins along the Mediterranean coast of modern Syria were discovered by accident. The excavation of the site, the ancient city of Ugarit, the following year led to the discovery of a large number of texts in an unknown script. When the script was deciphered, the language turned out to be very close to biblical Hebrew. The texts have added enormously to our knowledge of Canaanite religion and its connections to early Israelite religion. Before their discovery, most of our knowledge of Canaanite religion came from the Hebrew Scriptures—hardly an unbiased source—and a few scattered references in inscriptions and Egyptian writings. Even though Ugarit was further north than Israel, these texts comprise the most complete source of information on pre-Israelite Canaanite religion.

A number of scholars have studied the Ugaritic literature in depth. Influential early work was done by Cyrus Gordon, who studied the Ugaritic language and poetry,[22] and Mitchell Dahood, who studied the literature in connection with the Hebrew psalms and found many similarities in vocabulary, poetic techniques, and divine imagery.[23] On a more popular level is P. Craigie's *Ugarit and the Old Testament.*[24] Today nearly every study of early Israelite religion and language makes extensive use of comparison to the Ugaritic material. A good review of current study in the area is the *Anchor Bible Dictionary* article by D. Pardee and Pierre Bordreuil, "Ugarit (Texts and Literature)."[25]

The Ugaritic tablets were written around the fourteenth century B.C.E. and include a variety of letters, commercial texts, literary works and religious epics. The religious epics are particularly useful for Old Testament studies. The gods Baal and Asherah, condemned in the Old Testament, are major characters in the epics, as are the chief god El; Anat, the wife and sister of Baal; and numerous minor gods.[26]

The Ugaritic tablets do not tell us anything directly about the origin of the Israelites. Although neither the Israelites nor Yahweh are ever mentioned in the texts, they can indirectly help us answer the question of the origin of the Israelites. The texts include much information on Canaanite religion that was previously unknown—they were written shortly before Israel emerged. By comparing the Canaanite religion known from the Ugaritic texts to the earliest written expressions of Israelite religion, we can see how similar the two are: The earliest Israelite religion being markedly different from Canaanite religion would indicate that the first Israelites came to Canaan from the outside, but close similarities between the two would suggest that the first Israelites were indigenous to Canaan.

The chief god in the Ugaritic epics is El. El presides over the assembly of the gods, and other gods come to beg permission from El for any major undertaking. El is called "Bull El" and "Father." El has the assistance and adoration of the other gods, including his consort Asherah.[27] One passage gives an example of the relationships between El, his wife Asherah, and Baal and his wife and sister Anat.

> She [Asherah] puts fire on the brazier,
> A pot upon the coals
> And propitiates Bull El Benign,
> Does obeisance to the Creator of Creatures.
> Lifting up her eyes she beholds.
> The advance of Baal Asherah doth espy,
> The advance of the Maiden Anath....
> After this goes Puissant Baal,
> Also goes the Maiden Anath.
> As they do homage to Lady Asherah of the Sea,
> Obeisance to the Progenitress of the Gods,
> Quoth Lady Asherah of the Sea:
> Why do ye homage to Lady Asherah of the Sea
> Obeisance to the Progenitress of the Gods?
> Have you done homage to Bull El Benign,
> Or obeisance to the Creator of Creatures?[28]

The passage shows El receiving the highest worship, but Asherah is also given high honor by the other gods who come to ask permission from El to build a house for Baal.

Baal is also an important god in the Ugaritic epics. In fact, he is a more active character than El, is involved in the affairs of Earth more closely and is often at war with other gods, especially Yamm/Nahar (Sea/River—not two gods, but two names for the same god) and Mot (Death). Baal is called "Rider of the Clouds" and dwells on Mount Zaphon. His powerful voice is able to shake mountains. In this passage, he is assisted by minor divinities providing weapons for him in a battle with Yamm/Nahar.

> Now thine enemy, O Baal,
> Now thine enemy wilt thou smite,
> Now wilt thou cut off thine adversary.
> Thou'lt take thine eternal kingdom,

Thine everlasting dominion.
Kothar brings down two clubs....
The club swoops in the hand of Baal,
Like an eagle between his fingers;
It strikes the back of Prince Yamm,
Between the arms of Judge Nahar.
Yamm is firm; he is not bowed;
His joints bend not,
Nor breaks his frame.
Kothar brings down two clubs....
The club swoops in the hands of Baal,
Like an eagle between his fingers;
It strikes the pate of Prince Yamm,
Between the eyes of Judge Nahar.
Yamm collapses,
He falls to the ground;
His joints bend;
His frame breaks.[29]

Another minor Canaanite god who acted as assistant to Baal was Resheph (or Rashpu). In an inscription of uncertain date, not part of the Ugaritic texts, Reseph is mentioned in connection with the dedication of a city, along with Baal.

I have built this city. I have given it the name Azitawaddiya, for Ba'l and Reshef-*Sprm* commissioned me to build it. I have built it, by virtue of Ba'l and by virtue of Reshef-*Sprm,* with plenty to eat and well-being and in a good situation and in peace of mind....[30]

This is far from a complete description of Canaanite religion but enough of a representative sample to compare to descriptions of early Hebrew religion. Before getting into a specific comparison of the imagery and roles of the gods, note that the poetic techniques used in the Ugaritic epics is similar to that used in Hebrew poetry. The most obvious is parallelism, in which a line is followed by one that is almost synonymous. For example:

> Asherah propitiates Bull El Benign
> Does obeisance to the Creator of Creatures.

Note also this typical example from the Hebrew Bible:

> The voice of the Lord breaks the cedars;
> The Lord breaks the cedars of Lebanon. (Ps 29:5)

The vocabulary of the Ugaritic religious epics is also similar to that of the Hebrew Bible; Ugaritic is a language closely related to Hebrew. (Regardless of any religious similarity, the fact that Hebrew is a Canaanite language closely related to other Canaanite languages may suggest that the Israelites were indigenous to Canaan.)

Beyond the poetic techniques and vocabulary, the imagery used to describe the Canaanites gods is often similar to the Hebrew Bible's portrayals of Yahweh. In *The Early History of God: Yahweh and Other Deities in Ancient Israel,* Mark S. Smith discusses these similarities.[31] Yahweh has many characteristics in common with El. Like El, Yahweh is the chief god, creator of all. Like El, Yahweh is sometimes called "Father:" "He shall cry to me, You are my Father, my God, and the Rock of my salvation" (Ps 89:26). Just as El was called "Bull," often a bull or calf was used to represent the God of the Israelites (see Ex 32; 1 Kgs 12:25–33 and the archaeological information below).

Yahweh also has characteristics in common with Baal. The similarities between the imagery for Yahweh and the imagery for Baal are most pronounced in some of the earliest Hebrew poetry. It is difficult to date Hebrew poetry with certainty, but F. M. Cross, D. N. Freedman and others have found that the archaic features of form and vocabulary in Deuteronomy 33, Judges 5 and Habakkuk 3 place these texts among the earliest written expressions of Israelite religion, possibly having been composed before the year 1000 B.C.E.[32]

Some key verses from Deuteronomy 33 read:

The Lord came from Sinai
and dawned from Seir upon us;
he shone forth from Mount Paran.
With him were myriads of holy ones....(33:2)

There is none like God, O Jeshurun,
Who rides through the heavens to your help,
majestic through the skies.
He subdues the ancient gods,
shatters the forces of old;
He drove out the enemy before you,
and said, "Destroy!" (33:26–27)

Like Baal coming forth from Mount Zaphon, Yahweh comes from a mountain, either Sinai or Seir and Paran near the south end of the Dead Sea. Like the minor gods who assist Baal, Yahweh has "myriads of holy ones" for his battle. Like Baal, the "Rider of the Clouds," Yahweh rides through the heavens, and like Baal battling to victory against other gods, Yahweh subdues the ancient gods.

Judges 5 reads, in part:

Lord, when you went out from Seir,
When you marched from the region of Edom,
the earth trembled and the heavens poured,
the clouds indeed poured water.
The mountains quaked before the Lord, the one of Sinai,
before the Lord, the God of Israel. (5:4–5)

The stars fought from heaven,
from their courses they fought against Sisera. (5:20)

Like Baal shaking the mountains, Yahweh's coming shakes the mountains. Yahweh also has supernatural forces helping him in the battle—the stars from heaven.

Habakkuk 3 includes even more specific similarities to the Ugaritic descriptions of Baal:

God came from Teman,
the Holy One from Mount Paran.
His glory covered the heavens,
and the earth was full of his praise. (3:3)

Before him went pestilence [Deber],
And plague [Resheph] followed close behind.
He stopped and shook the earth;
he looked and made the nations tremble.
The eternal mountains were shattered;
along his ancient pathways
the everlasting hills sank low. (3:5–6)

Was your wrath against the rivers [Nahar], O Lord?
Or your anger against the rivers, [Nahar],
Or your rage against the sea, [Yam]
When you drove your horses, your chariots to victory? (3:8)

Like Baal, Yahweh comes from a mountain, again from the region south of the Dead Sea; again, the mountains and earth shake at his coming. More specifically, the god Resheph accompanies Yahweh. Although English translations usually treat the word in a naturalistic way *(plague)*, it may originally have been a reference to the same Canaanite god who is sometimes associated with Baal. Deber may also have been such a reference. Yahweh's enemy in this battle is Yam/Nahar, the very enemy Baal fights in the Ugaritic epics.

Another similarity between Israelite religion and Canaanite religion noted by Mark Smith is the role of Asherah. In the Ugaritic epics she is the consort of the chief god, El. There is good evidence that Asherah was treated as the consort of the chief Israelite god, Yahweh. The prophetic condemnations of worship of Asherah in the Old Testament have been supplemented by archaeological discoveries of inscriptions in Israel, mentioning "Yahweh and his Asherah," as if Asherah were Yahweh's consort (discussed more fully below).[33]

Besides the similarity in divine imagery and roles, there are other points of similarity between the Hebrew Scriptures and the Ugaritic literature. The best known is the mention of the wise man Daniel (or Danel) in both Ugaritic literature and the Bible. In the Ugaritic *Tale of Aqhat,* Daniel is the legendary father of Aqhat.[34] Besides becoming a legendary figure in the Old Testament book named after him, Daniel is mentioned in the Book of Ezekiel as a well-known wise man: "You are indeed wiser than Daniel; no secret is hidden from you" (28:3).

Psalm 29 has often been cited, particularly by Mitchell Dahood, as a hymn with many Ugaritic characteristics.[35] It is a psalm about Yahweh enthroned as king and has geographical references commonly used in Ugaritic texts (e.g., Lebanon). It also has grammatical similarities to Ugaritic hymns and concludes with a blessing similar to Ugaritic blessings: "May the Lord give strength to his people! May the Lord bless his people with peace!"[36]

There are many other parallels between Ugaritic religion and early Israelite religion, especially in the Psalms and in the idea of the Assembly of the Gods.[37] These examples are enough to show that the relationship was close. Evidently as Yahweh became the chief God of the Israelites, he took on characteristics of both El and Baal, including having El's consort Asherah as his own. The reason for this development can be accounted for in a number of ways, but it seems to be more than a borrowing by one group of another group's religious imagery. The similarities in language, poetic techniques, imagery, and roles of the gods are so close that they add support to theories contending that the first Israelites were indigenous to Canaan and not a group migrating in from the outside.

Part II: Archaeological Evidence

Archaeology is the study of the material remains of past peoples. It often tells us things we would never know from written sources alone. Archaeology studies everyday objects and structures that people took for granted and may never have bothered to write about, such as cooking vessels or the shapes and sizes of the rooms in their homes. Such studies can tell us much about how a people lived. They can also reveal connections between various peoples; for example, if several cities over a large area used identically decorated pottery, some social, economic or religious connection existed that led to the shared material culture.

Archaeology has its limits. Not very many objects used by ancient peoples are still around these two or three thousand years later. We do not have representative samples of most ancient material cultures, except for some items made of durable materials like stone or metal, as well as those objects fortunate enough to end up in places protected from deterioration by weather. However, archaeological evidence also does not come labeled. A square building with two rooms and one door could be a house, or it could be a shrine. A wall showing evidence of destruction doesn't tell us who destroyed it or why. In sites occupied over several centuries, it is not always easy to separate all of the remains into correct chronological layers. Archaeology does not answer every question we have, but it can tell us a great deal, especially today, when it is done in association with anthropology, sociology and the natural sciences.

There are several recent works that provide an overview of the archaeology of early Israel. Among the best are Amihai Mazar's *Archaeology of the Land of the Bible, 10,000–586 B.C.E.;*[38] William Dever's *Recent Archaeological Discoveries and Biblical Research;*[39] Israel Finkelstein's *Archaeology of the Israelite Settlement;*[40] and *The Archaeology of Ancient Israel,* edited by A. Ben-Tor, which includes chapters by several leading archaeologists.[41]

A. Canaanite Cities

Because the biblical story is about a military conquest of the land of Canaan, and because some scholars have used archaeological evidence to support the historicity of the conquest, a good place to start to examine the archaeological evidence is the Canaanite cities. If there was such a conquest as that which the Book of Joshua describes, with many large cities destroyed in a unified invasion, then there should be archaeological evidence of the destruction. A large number of Canaanite cities have been excavated, but the evidence needed to indicate what happened to those cities around the years 1200–1000 B.C.E. is mixed.

One thing that is clear is that there was a decline in the overall system of fortified Canaanite cities. Mazar and Dever show that some of the cities were indeed destroyed, including some that the Book of Joshua claims the Israelites conquered, such as Hazor, Lachish and Bethel. But other cities that Joshua claims were destroyed, including Jericho and Ai, show no evidence of even being inhabited at the time. Other cities were destroyed but not all at the same time, so it is unlikely that their destructions were from a single cause. Other cities were not destroyed at all, but they seem to have lost population during Iron Age I.[42]

There was a gradual decline of the Canaanite cities, but the evidence does not support a unified military invasion of Canaan. Why the decline occurred is not certain. There may have been a decline in Egyptian strength, which in the past had provided stability to Canaan; there may have been more fighting among the cities themselves; there may have been an increase in raids by the *hapiru;* there may have been severe economic decline caused by several poor harvests. Most likely, a combination of factors led to the gradual decline of the Canaanite cities.

B. New Settlements in Iron Age I

While the old Canaanite cities were declining, a number of new settlements were established in the hill country of Canaan. Mazar provides descriptions of the new settlements. The Canaanite cities tended to be along the coast or close to the interior valleys with the best agricultural land. The new villages were in the poorer, hillier land. They were also small, many of them with a population of less than one hundred. Most of the new settlements were not fortified with walls around them but were simply collections of houses. In some cases the houses were arranged roughly in a circle to provide some defense or possibly to enclose livestock. The houses of a village were usually the same approximate size, indicating a society less stratified into social classes than the Canaanite cities were. Frequently, pits for grain storage were found with the houses.[43]

There was some regional variation among these new settlements. According to Adam Zertal, in the territory of Manasseh (central Canaan) the first new settlements were located in places where the inhabitants depended on perennial water sources under control of the Canaanite cities that were still existing, indicating a time of peaceful coexistence.[44] Elsewhere the settlements were more removed from the Canaanite cities.

The establishment of new settlements in the hill country at the beginning of Iron Age I was not a unique event. Finkelstein draws attention to the fact that in Early Bronze Age I (3300–3050 B.C.E.) and Middle Bronze Age II B–C (1800–1550 B.C.E.), there had been periods of settlement in the highlands, followed by periods of no occupation.[45] The reasons for the new settlements were not necessarily the same in every case, but this evidence does remind us to broaden our perspective and to compare the beginnings of Israel to similar changes in the region at other times.

These new settlements are often referred to as Israelite settlements, but archaeologists are cautious about making the identification. It is true that the new villages represent the appearance of a new social system at the time that Israel was emerging in the land of Canaan. We know from the Merneptah Stele that there were at least some people in Canaan known as Israelites by this time. It is true that the small villages fit very well the biblical picture of a decentralized, tribal society. But ethnic identification based on material remains is not always possible. It cannot be certain that at the time the new villages were established, the inhabitants would have identified themselves as Israelites. It is best to say that there was a transition in Canaan that resulted in the appearance of new villages and that these villages eventually took on a common identity as the collective home of the people who came to be known as the Israelites.

C. House Types

A common type of house found in many of the new settlements has become known as the four-room house, although the number of rooms actually varies. The four-room house typically is a rectangular structure with a single door at one side. There is a central, unroofed courtyard and stone pillars or wooden posts supporting a roof for side rooms. Across the back is one broad room. There may have been a second story in some cases, or at least the roof may have been used for sleeping in warm weather.[46]

The four-room house is so common in the new settlements that it is sometimes taken as an identifying characteristic of Israelite material culture. But there is some evidence that the four-room house is modeled after Canaanite architecture; similar houses have been found in Late Bronze Age Canaanite cities, and examples have been found in Philistine cities and in non-Israelite settlements east of the Jordan River.[47] To be sure, the overall architecture of the new villages is different from that of the large Canaanite cities; for example, the new villages do not have large public buildings and lack variety in types of buildings. Some archaeologists, such as Volkmar Fritz, do not believe that the four-room house is a continuation of the Canaanite-style house but represents a new type;[48] however, the typical dwellings of these settlements do bear enough similarities to the Canaanite houses to suggest to many archaeologists a connection between the old Canaanite cities and the new settlements.

D. Pottery

Pottery is one of the most valuable artifacts that archaeologists use for dating and identifying a site's material culture. For one thing, there was so much of it: Cooking vessels, storage vessels and religious articles were all of pottery. Also, broken pottery was commonly discarded in fill levels beneath new construction, and such broken pieces can last a very long time. The style of pottery was constantly changing, but at any given time there was great uniformity in a people's style of pottery (much like fashions in clothes today). Because of these characteristics, the pottery of a site is extremely useful for dating the site and determining which group of people lived there.

As with the houses, there is a common type of pottery found in many of the new settlements of Iron Age I. The common pottery of the period is called *collared rim,* because there is usually a ridge, or collar, around the base of the neck. The collared-rim jar was once thought to be distinctively Israelite, but examples have been found in Canaanite cities. The pottery of most of the new settlements is similar to Canaanite pottery, but it tends to be cruder and less varied in design, with an emphasis on utility rather than decorative features.[49]

The significance of the pottery can be interpreted in different ways. To some, such as Mazar, it indicates that the inhabitants of the new settlements were outsiders who had migrated into the land and had no pottery tradition of their own. When they began to make pottery, they imitated the styles of the nearby Canaanites, but because it was new to them their pieces were simpler and cruder.[50] Others, including Dever, say the pottery indicates that the people in the settlements were Canaanites, continuing to make the pottery they were used to. But the lifestyle of the people in the new villages would have demanded a more utilitarian assemblage of pottery. Also, unlike those of the Canaanite cities, where there would have been skilled specialists making and selling pottery to all, the inhabitants in the small settlements would have made their own pottery, so the forms are simpler than those found in the Canaanite cities.[51]

There is also regional variation in the pottery among the new settlements. Collared-rim jars were most common in the central regions, but Rafael Frankel points out that in the Upper Galilee the collared-rim jars were not found.[52] A. Kempinski, in studying southern Judah, found a mixture of pottery at Tel Masos, including Canaanite and Philistine vessels of the earliest phase (end of the thirteenth or early twelfth century B.C.E.) and Midianite and Phoenician vessels of the second phase, near the end of the eleventh century B.C.E.[53] The variations suggest that the people in the new settlements may not have all had the same origin.

E. Religious Objects and Sites in the New Settlements

Another type of archaeological evidence is religious artifacts. Shrines, statues, altars and other religious items, including items for household use, are part of a people's material culture. The material remains of religious practices do not always give us an accurate idea of the beliefs and spiritual values associated with the objects, but as part of a people's material remains, they can indicate connections among groups of peoples. A similarity between the religious objects used by the Israelites and the ones used by Canaanites suggests continuity between the two groups. Complete difference between the objects suggests that the Israelites came to Canaan from the outside.

The discussion above on the Ugaritic texts indicated that early Israelite religion was similar to Canaanite religion in terms of the literary imagery used to describe God. The Old Testament, especially the prophetic books, frequently condemns the Israelites for worshiping other gods, particularly the gods of the Canaanites. The archaeological evidence shows that the prophets were not exaggerating when they looked upon almost everyone in the nation as habitual worshipers of other gods besides Yahweh. The material remains indicate a close connection between the Canaanite and Israelite religions.

The new settlements did not leave behind large temples or even a large number of religious objects. That itself could indicate a nomadic background; perhaps the inhabitants were not accustomed to building permanent shrines. One object, though, is of particular interest: A. Mazar studied an open high place in Samaria, near several of the new settlements, where a religious site was discovered, including a circle of stones and a place for making offerings. A bronze statue of a bull, about 18 centimeters long, was found at the site—bulls were often associated with the Canaanite gods El and Baal—and bronze statues of bulls have been found at the Canaanite cities of Hazor and Ugarit. The location of this find in the midst of the new villages convinced Mazar that it was a worship site for people of the villages.[54] If Israelite worship at such places was widespread, it would explain the biblical condemnations of going to the "high places" and the condemnations of the golden calf (Ex 32) and the bulls at the temples of Dan and Bethel (1 Kgs 12).

At Kuntillet 'Ajrud, in the Negev, a religious site was discovered that apparently had served as a pilgrimage shrine. Ze'ev Meshel excavated the shrine and dated it to the late ninth or early eighth century B.C.E. Several inscriptions were also discovered at the shrine, including some that speak of "Yahweh and his Asherah," as if the Canaanite goddess Asherah were a consort of Yahweh.[55] Although the site is later than the beginnings of Israel, it indicates that the worship of Canaanite gods by Israelites during the tribal period continued to thrive in the monarchy. At Khirbet el-Qom, west of Hebron, an inscription was discovered that also mentioned Asherah. The interpretation of this inscription is more uncertain than the one from Kuntillet 'Ajrud, but it does add support to the view that the Canaanite goddess Asherah was worshiped for centuries by the Israelites.[56] In a detailed study of the worship of Asherah in Israel, Saul Olyan concluded that during the monarchy, worship of Asherah was associated with worship of Yahweh in both the northern and southern kingdoms and in both official religion and popular piety. Only toward the end of the monarchy was there an attempt (by the Deuteronomic movement) to treat worship of Asherah as something foreign.[57]

Also, numerous figurines have been discovered from Judean houses up to the end of the monarchy. The figurines have been identified as fertility goddesses and apparently were commonly used as part of household piety. They bear a resemblance to Late Bronze Age Canaanite figurines.[58]

The worship of other gods, particularly Canaanite gods, remained a widespread part of Israelite religion through the tribal and monarchy periods. Although the Old Testament calls this a borrowing of foreign gods, it is also possible that the Israelites worshiped Canaanite gods because most of them had, in fact, been Canaanites.

F. The Philistine Cities

The Philistines, one of the groups of Sea Peoples in the texts discussed above, are also known through archaeological evidence from the cities they established in Canaan. The Old Testament refers to the Philistine pentapolis, the five cities of Gaza, Ashdod, Ashkelon, Ekron and Gath. Excavations of Ashdod, Ashkelon, Ekron (Tel Miqne) and other sites give a picture of Philistine material culture at the time of their arrival in Canaan and the next several centuries. The material culture shows influence from the Aegean region, from Egypt and from their Canaanite and Israelite neighbors.

Trude and Moshe Dothan found that the pottery from the earliest time periods at Philistine sites was similar to that from the Aegean, especially from Mycenae. There was also evidence of influence from Cyprus (which itself had Mycenaean influence). In the later levels of occupation, Philistine pottery became more like Canaanite and Israelite pottery.[59] The Dothans concluded that the Philistines had originally come from somewhere in the Aegean, migrated to Cyprus and then moved to Canaan. When they first settled in Canaan the Philistines continued to make pottery according to their earlier customs but gradually adopted the material culture of the Canaanites and Israelites around them.[60]

Burial customs also showed a mixed influence. At some sites Philistines were buried in "anthropoid" coffins—clay human-shaped coffins with lids depicting human faces. These coffins were similar to Egyptian coffins.[61] At Azor, a village near modern Tel Aviv, Philistines were buried in the ground in individual burials, along with pottery and other offerings, from about 1100 B.C.E. At that time individual burial was not practiced among the Canaanites but was beginning to be practiced in the Aegean, indicating a connection with that region.[62] Also at Azor, evidence of cremation was found. Cremation was not practiced by Canaanites but was practiced at a few places in Greece, again indicating a connection with that region.[63]

Philistine religious sites and objects also showed mixed influence. At Tell Qasile, a Philistine site within the modern city of Tel Aviv, three phases of a temple were discovered. Although it has no exact parallels, it had several similarities in layout to temples in Mycenae and Cyprus and some similarities to Canaanite temples in Lachish and Beth Shean. Cult stands at the temple were borrowed from the Canaanite tradition, and pottery showed Egyptian influence.[64] At Ashdod, a figurine in the shape of a seated goddess was discovered that resembled figurines from the Aegean.[65] At Ashdod, Azor and other sites, several figurines of mourning women with their hands on their heads were discovered, also similar to Aegean figurines.[66]

The archaeological evidence of mixed influences might at first seem to complicate things, but along with the texts, gives us a likely picture for the background of the Philistines. They were part of a wave of migrants from the Aegean in the thirteenth and twelfth centuries B.C.E. Egypt tried to keep them out of the lands they controlled but were not completely successful and hired some as mercenaries for their fortresses in Canaan. As Egyptian power declined, the Philistines were able to establish an independent league of cities in Canaan. In time, they became the chief enemy of the emerging Israelites, but they also began to adopt the material culture and religious traditions of the Canaanites and Israelites.

This review of literary and archaeological evidence does not answer every question about the origin of the Israelites; it does, however, give us some insights on the two issues mentioned at the beginning of the chapter, namely, whether there was continuity or discontinuity between the Israelites and the Canaanites and whether the beginning of Israel was a peaceful or a violent process. The evidence shows close similarity between the two groups in both religious imagery and archaeological remains. The differences in pottery and house types are minor and are interpreted differently among scholars in the field. In an article thoroughly examining the archaeological evidence, Gloria London concluded that the variations can be explained by the different requirements of urban and rural living and that the similarities are strong enough to support the idea that the Canaanites and the Israelites should not be considered two different peoples.[67] As we will see, though, others claim that even minor differences in the material remains can be clues that the ancestors of the Israelites were distinct from those of the Canaanites.

The evidence also suggests that it was largely a peaceful process. There are indications of occasional violence but no substantial proof that the incidents of violence that did occur all came from the same cause. Any of the theories could account for occasional violence; the Canaanite cities fought against each other, and the Egyptians and Philistines both had designs on the land. But virtually all scholars agree that the explanation for the origin of the Israelites should not include the complete conquest of one nation by another.

3
Three Classic Models

During the first three-quarters of the twentieth century, biblical scholars and archaeologists who debated the question of the origin of the Israelites developed three competing models to explain Israelite beginnings. Although most scholars today do not accept any of the models in the exact forms in which they were originally proposed, it is useful in discussing this issue to review these three models before looking at the most recent positions. Much of the search for archaeological and literary evidence has been influenced by a desire to prove or disprove one or another of the models, and many recent views are variations of or responses to the three classic theories.

These three models are explanations of who the majority of the first Israelites were. All three acknowledge that there were additional people from various backgrounds who joined with the early Israelites. The biblical story itself describes a mixed multitude joining the Israelites as they left Egypt (Ex 12:38). It also states that some of the people living in Canaan joined them, including the family of Rahab in Jericho (Jos 2; 6) and the Gibeonites (Jos 9). These models do not try to account for every last person who became part of the Israelites but are attempts to describe the major process that led to a change in the land of Canaan—from the system of Egyptian-ruled Canaanite city-states to a decentralized system of small villages in the highlands.

Conquest—W. F. Albright

The Conquest model most closely follows the biblical story, although scholars who supported it did not take every detail of the biblical story as literally true. In one sense this model can be considered the earliest because in its nonscholarly form it is simply the assumption that the Bible correctly records ancient history and is thus close to what many people have traditionally believed about the Bible. But scholars who developed this model were in part reacting against the trend to find historical explanations completely different from the biblical story. This model was an attempt to show that using all the critical means available did not have to mean rejecting the basics of the biblical story.

W. F. Albright, an American archaeologist working in the first half of the twentieth century, was mainly responsible for articulating the Conquest model and finding archaeological support for it. For Albright, the Israelites were a people religiously and ethnically distinct from the Canaanites, whose religion he described as "crude and depraved."[1] According to his theory, the story in the Pentateuch and Joshua is based on underlying history; the Israelites came out of slavery in Egypt and, after some years of migration through the desert, invaded Canaan from the east. Albright acknowledged that the story may exaggerate some of Joshua's military exploits and that other people, from both inside and outside of Canaan, joined the Israelites. But the main process was a successful military invasion by a unified people distinct from the Canaanites.

Albright cited archaeological evidence to support the historicity of the conquest. He pointed to excavations of several large Canaanite cities that showed evidence of destruction at the end of the Late Bronze Age, including Debir, Bethel, Hazor and Lachish.[2] Even cities that other archaeologists claimed were not inhabited at the time of the supposed conquest, such as Jericho and Ai, could fit Albright's theory, he claimed. At Jericho there did not appear to be any evidence of habitation in the Late Bronze Age, but Albright explained this by saying that most of the evidence of Late-Bronze-

Age habitation had eroded away. Albright claimed that the biblical story of the conquest of Ai, another place that showed no evidence of habitation, was a transferred story that originally was about nearby Bethel.[3]

There has, of course, been much archaeological research since Albright's time, and much of the evidence he used is no longer considered valid, but his views continued to be influential for many years. Fundamentalists, ignoring the nuances of his views, have cited him as proof that the Bible is historically accurate.[4] His views have been followed by conservative Scripture scholars wanting to view the Bible as historically accurate. Even those who disagreed with his views spent a great deal of time responding to his arguments.

Peaceful Infiltration—Albrecht Alt

When modern biblical scholarship cast doubts on the historicity of the Pentateuch and Joshua's account of Israel's beginnings, scholars naturally began to look for alternative explanations. The explanation that caught on among a large number of scholars became known as the Peaceful Infiltration theory. Simply put, this theory maintains that the early Israelites were nomads from the surrounding regions who gradually and peacefully began to settle in the highlands of Canaan. As these settlements increased, there were occasional battles between the new Israelites and the Canaanite cities, and as the cities declined and Egypt lost control of Canaan, the new Israelite settlers became the dominant force in the land of Canaan.

The German Scripture scholar Albrecht Alt was mainly responsible for developing this model. According to Alt, the stories in Genesis about Abraham, Isaac and Jacob preserve some genuine historical memories of the nomadic people who became the Israelites. These nomads, or seminomads, had migrated into and out of Canaan on a seasonal basis long before they settled in permanent villages. The tribes who did settle in Canaan included previously unrelated tribes from various directions. They had previously worshiped different gods, who are reflected in the different titles used for God in the stories of the patriarchs. At first they settled in the empty spaces away from the Canaanite cities, that is, in the highlands. With the decline of the Canaanite city-state system, they were able to occupy the lowlands as well.[5]

Alt's model was closely followed by Martin Noth in his history of Israel. According to Noth, the Israelites could not have been indigenous to Canaan because the location of their settlements—in the hill country away from the Canaanite cities—and their way of living clearly indicate patterns of peaceful migration and the preservation of desert tribal traditions.[6] The patriarchal stories may preserve some history, but they are mainly the cumulative result of a common coexistence spanning several generations in Palestine and attest to the human desire of the inhabitants to formulate a common history expressing their relatedness.[7] Noth says that it is impossible to date the migrations into Canaan precisely but that they must have begun around the end of the fourteenth century B.C.E. and were finished by 1100 B.C.E.[8]

The Peaceful Infiltration model appealed to people who were convinced that a more gradual process best explained the beginnings of the Israelites, and it is also more compatible with the idea that the Israelites came from mixed backgrounds. The model originally did not make use of much archaeological data, but there are several scholars today who believe that a modified version of this theory is supported by archaeological evidence.

Social Revolution—George Mendenhall and Norman Gottwald

Beginning in the 1960s, a third model was developed, first by George Mendenhall and then by Norman Gottwald. This model, usually called Peasant Revolt in the past, maintains that most of the early Israelites were not people who came into Canaan from elsewhere but were indigenous Canaanites. The lower-class Canaanites were heavily taxed by the Canaanite kings and had little control over their own lives, so they finally rose up in a violent revolt. The revolt was successful, and these people then established a new decentralized, egalitarian society in the highlands.

In a 1962 article, Mendenhall discussed the phenomenon of people politically separating themselves from the dominant rule in Canaan. The Amarna letters (discussed in chapter 2) were written by Canaanite kings to their Egyptian rulers during the fourteenth century B.C.E. and mention a people called the *hapiru*. These *hapiru* had politically separated themselves from the city-state society and lived as outlaws in the countryside. There was thus a precedent for some form of social upheaval occurring in Canaan shortly before the beginnings of Israel. Some two centuries later, when the situation was still oppressive for lower-class Canaanites, would not be the first time that Canaanites revolted against their rulers to live more independently.

Mendenhall put much emphasis on the possibility of there being some history behind the Exodus and wandering in the wilderness stories and held that the religious views of the people involved were shaped by these experiences. The Exodus group believed that they were in a special relationship with a God who delivers the oppressed from their oppressors. When these Israelites of the Exodus entered Canaan, Canaanites dissatisfied with the rule of the cities did what the *hapiru* had done earlier—they withdrew, except that this time they joined forces with the Israelites. This new community became united by developing a shared religion with a God who saved the oppressed from the powerful.[9]

In subsequent years, Norman Gottwald developed this model in much more detail. His 1979 book, *The Tribes of Yahweh: A Sociology of the Religion of Liberated Israel, 1250–1050 B.C.E.,* combined extensive analyses of texts and archaeological data with a sociological study of changing societies.[10] Gottwald focused more on the internal process, the role of the lower-class Canaanites themselves, and less on the Exodus group inspiring them to revolt. After describing the Egyptian-ruled feudal system of the Canaanite city-states, he said that by the thirteenth century

B.C.E., there were several rural groups with converging interests. The *hapiru,* the peasant farmers, the *shasu* and other nomads all wanted more economic and political independence from the city-states.[11] These groups were not united until Israel emerged as a growing coalition of people opposed to the city-states. Prior to this, Israel consisted of a group of rural inhabitants within Canaan who later began to worship Yahweh when the small Exodus group joined them. The unity provided by a common worship of Yahweh was thus instrumental in forming these people of diverse backgrounds into a unified people.[12]

The Social Revolution model has been criticized for going too far beyond the evidence and for imposing modern ideology, particularly Marxist ideology, on the process. But it has been influential in leading biblical scholars to make more use of the social sciences and to focus attention on the Canaanites themselves as the possible people from which Israel emerged.

Evaluation of the Models

These three classic models are in sharp disagreement with one another. While they may agree on some details, there are two major issues on which they differ. First, were the early Israelites indigenous to Canaan, or were they people who came from elsewhere? The Conquest and Peaceful Infiltration models maintain that they came from elsewhere; the Social Revolution model holds that they were Canaanites. Second, was the beginning of Israel mainly a violent or a peaceful process? The Conquest and Social Revolution models say it was violent; the Peaceful Infiltration model says it was mainly peaceful.

Archaeological and textual evidence discussed in the last chapter suggested that Israel's beginnings were mainly peaceful, with scattered violence from various causes. The evidence was mixed on whether the first Israelites were indigenous to Canaan or came from elsewhere, although the majority of archaeologists now believe they were indigenous to Canaan. Those who argue in favor of one or another of these models can, of course, come up with explanations as to why some of the evidence does not seem to fit; the models can also be revised slightly to take account of the recent evidence.

The three models are in disagreement to the extent that they attempt to explain the beginnings of the majority of the Israelites. It is possible, though, that the truth is in some combination of the models. If the people who eventually became Israel came from diverse backgrounds, it is possible that each model tells part of the story, but no one of them tells the whole story.

Conquest

The literary evidence of Joshua and Judges can be used to claim that some battles occurred at the time Israel was first emerging in Canaan. However, Joshua and Judges contradict each other, and an awareness of their theological purpose raises doubts about how much history they contain. The lack of evidence of uniform destruction of the Canaanite cities that the Book of Joshua attributes to the Israelites is a problem for this theory. Absence of evidence is not evidence of absence, but at this point it is difficult to accept the idea of a unified, successful conquest of the cities.

Because this model views the Israelites as a group distinct from the Canaanites and that came in from the outside, all of the evidence that suggests continuity between the Canaanites and the Israelites is hard for the Conquest view to explain. From the comparison of the Ugaritic texts to early Hebrew poetry, it is clear that the earliest written expressions of Israelite religion had much in common with Canaanite religion. Widespread worship of Canaanite gods continued for centuries in Israel. Analyses of house types and pottery also suggest continuity between Canaanites and Israelites, although there is some room for different interpretations of these. The Conquest model would have to posit an immediate adoption of Canaanite characteristics by the newly arrived Israelites.

Finally, the location of the new settlements is difficult for the Conquest model to explain. If a group of people came in from the outside and successfully defeated the previous inhabitants, they would be expected to take over the best land. The Canaanite cities were already around the best land, but the new settlements are in the poorer hill country.

The Conquest model is the one with the least evidence supporting it, and it has little scholarly support today.

Peaceful Infiltration

The location of the new settlements is consistent with this explanation. Nomadic people settling down in new villages would prefer taking unoccupied land, even if it was poorer, to meeting the more powerful Canaanites in battle. Archaeological evidence is also consistent with this model because it attests to a process of change brought about through occasional violence and destruction of cities from various causes rather than through a unified invasion. The new settlers may have had peaceful intents but found themselves at battle occasionally anyway; in addition, there were other groups around to account for battles near the cities.

A significant piece of evidence for this model is the presence of the *shasu* in the region. The *shasu,* mentioned frequently in Egyptian documents, could be the very people that the proponents of this theory claim migrated into Canaan. If it is true that some of the *shasu* worshiped Yahweh, this theory is strengthened considerably. The stories in Genesis of Abraham, Isaac and Jacob having a lifestyle similar to the *shasu* may support this model as well.

One difficulty for advocates of the Peaceful Infiltration model is explaining all of the evidence indicating continuity between the Canaanites and the Israelites. Like the Conquest version, this model claims a group other than the Canaanites came in from the outside. This model must explain the similarities in material culture and religion as an immediate adoption of Canaanite customs by the new arrivals or as a result of close contact between the nomads and the Canaanites before the nomads settled in the villages. Israel Finkelstein and Volkmar Fritz, whose views will be discussed in chapter 6, use the latter explanation in modified versions of this theory.[13]

The Infiltration theory also has to explain why the Bible tells a different story of Israelite origins. One can claim that the story of a gradual infiltration is preserved in an altered form in the stories in Genesis, but that still does not explain why the Exodus and conquest stories were used by people whose origins were entirely different.

Social Revolution

The Social Revolution model says the Israelites did not come in from the outside but were Canaanites themselves. Therefore the evidence of continuity adds support to this model. The evidence on the fate of the Canaanite cities is also consistent with this model. It is true that a revolt is a violent uprising and has much in common with an invasion, but a revolt is directed more at the people ruling than the buildings and walls of the cities. A revolt can be successful and yet leave behind only scattered evidence of destruction.

Like the Conquest theory, this model does need to explain why the new settlements were located in the poorer land. If these people successfully defeated the Canaanite kings, why did they not take over the best land? Possible explanations are that the small villages in the hills were more suited to their egalitarian ideology and their determination not to have a single king ruling over them or that the people involved in the revolution came from a rural background and preferred to stay there. Still, explaining why the victors' ideology could not be put into practice on good agricultural land, if it was available through military conquest, is a difficulty with this model.

Supporters of this model also need to explain why the Bible tells such a different story. They can claim that the revolt at

Israel's beginnings *did* shape the Bible—in the laws on treating the poor, refugees, widows and orphans and in the negative attitude toward kings in much of the Old Testament. This model can also claim that the Exodus story was adopted by the people involved in the revolution because it expressed a similar idea of God rescuing the oppressed. But the event of a successful revolt, if it occurred, would seem to be the type of story that would support those teachings even more. It is difficult for this model to explain why that story disappeared.

All three classic models have weaknesses. Those who write histories of Israel often conclude that some combination of the models is a better answer or that we must wait for more evidence before trying to give a definitive answer. Some recent works also suggest other explanations to account for the emergence of the Israelites. Those explanations and how they might be compatible with parts of the other models I will consider in the next chapters.

4

The Peoples of Canaan at the Beginning of Iron Age I

Having seen the archaeological and literary evidence that scholars use to answer the question of the Israelites' origins and the earlier models that have been proposed, we can see that current views on the issue are built on the models of the past and on recent archaeological advances. But the current positions of scholars are built not only on raw data, but also on interpretations of that data into some coherent picture of Canaanite society and its interaction with other nearby peoples. The Israelites emerged in Canaan at the beginning of Iron Age I as part of the mix of different peoples living in the region. Scholars differ on the relationship between the Israelites and the Canaanites and how much of a role the *hapiru,* the *shasu* and the Sea Peoples had in shaping Israel's beginnings.

Before looking at the recent positions of scholars on the origin of the Israelites, it is necessary to have a clear idea of the identities of the Canaanites and the other people who lived in and around Canaan at the time Israel began. In this chapter I will look at the work of scholars who have tried not only to synthesize the data on Canaanite society, but also to render an overall picture of the people living in and around Canaan. When we have a clearer idea of the Canaanites and the people around them at the beginning of Iron

Age I, then we will be in a better position to understand the emergence of the Israelites.

The Land of Canaan

Our first step toward better understanding the Canaanites and their neighbors is to determine how the word *Canaan* was used in ancient times. I am not concerned here with the etymology of the word *Canaan,* but to what territory and people it referred. Niels Peter Lemche has attempted to answer that in *The Canaanites and Their Land: The Tradition of the Canaanites.*[1] In examining the Amarna letters, he concludes that the letters do not designate a precise territory for Canaan. In part, this was because the writers assumed that the readers of the letters knew where Canaan was and thus did not bother to explain it. But more important are what seem like contradictions in the letters: for example, Ugarit is sometimes referred to as if it were part of Canaan and other times as if it were not.[2] Lemche explains that most people in ancient times did not have our notions of ethnicity and nationality. Political control over an area might change frequently, and a group of people with similar cultural traditions, language and religion might never be politically unified under one king. The group that a person would have been considered a part of would have been a matter of perspective. It would not have been strange for a person who did not think of him- or herself as a Canaanite to be considered a Canaanite by others. (The question of ethnicity is a difficult one, and I will look at some of the recent positions on this issue in later chapters.)

In the Late Bronze Age and the beginning of Iron Age I, the word *Canaan* does refer in a general way to northern Palestine and Syria. Not everyone used it in the same exact sense, however, so it would be impossible to draw the precise boundaries of a political entity called Canaan. Also, because the material culture of the area is so similar to that of the Israelites who later inhabited much of what had been called Canaan, Lemche concludes that there is no such thing as a Canaanite religion or Canaanite culture distinct from Israelite religion and culture. All should be referred to as "Western Asiatic peoples."[3]

Of course, the Old Testament, written centuries later, does use the term *Canaanite* as if it were something entirely different from the word *Israelite*. Scholars recognize that that is an artificial distinction made for theological purposes. *Canaanite* became a negative term for those aspects of Palestinian religion that no longer had the approval of the Old Testament authors. The distinction between *Canaanite* and *Israelite* that biblical authors of the exile made later would not have been made at the beginnings of Israel.

The People in and around Canaan

The territory known as Canaan had a mixed population. There were the inhabitants of large, fortified cities. There were rural peasants under the control of the cities. There were the *hapiru,* on the fringes of Canaanite society but often involved in the affairs of the cities. There were a small number of people living in the highlands. There were nomads like the *shasu,* not permanently part of Canaan but living near and sometimes in, Canaan. By 1200 B.C.E. there is evidence of a group called Israel, and there were Philistines and other Sea Peoples arriving in Canaan.

The most complete body of evidence relates to the people in the cities. In chapter 2 we saw that the archaeological evidence from the cities, along with the written evidence, especially the Amarna letters, give us a good picture of the political and economic situation. The Canaanite cities were fortified, and the Amarna letters mention frequent battles. Part of the population must have been a full-time, professional army. The variety of house sizes indicates a stratified population; a ruling elite lived off the production of the lower classes. Pottery and other crafts show great skill, possibly indicating a class of specialized craftspeople. There would also have been a professional priesthood staffing the temples of the cities.

There is less evidence dealing with the lives of the rural Canaanite peasants. Farmers do not leave behind as much archaeological evidence as city dwellers. Norman Gottwald describes a feudal or "tributary" system, with the farmers giving all of their surplus to the rulers of the cities (who in turn had to pay high tribute to the Egyptians).[4] The Amarna letters mention raids on fields and villages by *hapiru* and neighboring kings. The rural people lived an insecure life, dependent on the protection of the king's army. They were thus caught between needing the protection of the city and resenting the control that the city had over them.

The *hapiru* were also part of Canaanite society. Even though they seem to be outcasts, their way of life was very much connected with the Canaanite cities. The degree of cooperation between *hapiru* and the kings varied. They were hired as mercenaries by the kings or raided places when they could. In some of the Amarna letters, Canaanite kings accuse other Canaanite kings of being in close alliance with the *hapiru;* Lab'ayu of Shechem, for example, was involved in controversies over being accused of cooperating with *hapiru.*[5] The *hapiru* included displaced people from the cities and farms and thus ethnically and religiously would have been indistinguishable from other Canaanites.

There were also a few people living in the more remote highlands, the territories where the later Israelite settlements emerged. There is archaeological evidence of a few villages, although not as many as there had been earlier in the Middle Bronze Age or would be later in Iron Age I.[6] David Hopkins, in a thorough study of the agricultural possibilities of the highlands, emphasizes the poor agricultural potential of those territories.[7] It would therefore have been less worthwhile for the Canaanite kings to try to control them as they did the better agricultural lands of the valleys. Also, the ruggedness of the highlands would have made it difficult for the chariot armies of the cities and the Egyptians to control the highlands. Who these scattered people were who lived in the highlands is not certain. They could have been *hapiru;* they could also have been nomadic people who settled down in villages. Gösta

Ahlström points out that there may have been many more nomadic people in the highlands than the archaeological evidence has revealed; the large number of goat bones discovered in places would indicate that there were nomads in the highlands, even though most of the evidence of their lives has disappeared.[8]

The *shasu* should also be mentioned in this mix of population. The *shasu* were not part of Canaan. The Egyptian texts mention encountering them in many places, most often around Edom, southeast of Canaan. However, they were close to and sometimes in Canaan. If they began to settle down in permanent villages, then it is likely that some of them were part of the mix of people who later became Israel. Some scholars, such as Donald Redford, believe they were the major part of what became Israel.[9]

The Philistines and other Sea Peoples were outsiders in this mix of people, ethnically distinct from the Canaanites. The textual evidence from Egypt and the archaeological evidence from Philistine cities, studied especially by Trude and Moshe Dothan, shows that they originally came from the Aegean region and migrated throughout the eastern Mediterranean in the thirteenth and twelfth centuries B.C.E. The Philistines who settled in Canaan became an independent nation and remained so for several centuries, although their material culture gradually conformed to that of the other people living in Canaan.

Political Circumstances

Norman Gottwald's analysis of the political system of Canaan at the end of the Late Bronze Age and the beginning of Iron Age I is that it was a loosely organized feudal system within the Egyptian empire. Egypt did not administer Canaan closely but depended on the local kings of the cities to rule their respective territories and to deliver tribute to Egypt. Egypt benefitted from the competition and political fragmentation that existed among the city-states because their disunity and overall weakness prevented them from rising against the Egyptian regime. The city-states benefitted from Egyptian power because it prevented any one city from dominating the others too much and provided enough stability for trade and economic prosperity to occur.[10]

The system thus depended on a balance of power among Egypt and the numerous cities. That balance varied from place to place. Egypt was able to exert the most effective control in the coastal plains and internal valleys, including parts of the Jordan valley—those places most accessible to their chariot forces. Cities in the highlands felt less Egyptian control but in turn had less power over their own scattered rural populations.[11] The various rural people—peasant farmers, *hapiru* and nomads—had little political power but benefitted from a stable situation, as long as that stability did not come at the cost of oppression and poverty.

Changes in the Early Iron Age

Part of the puzzle surrounding the origin of the Israelites relates to why the stability provided by Egypt came to an end. The weakening of Egyptian power after long years of fighting the Hittites, dissatisfaction among rural and other lower-class people in Canaan and the arrival of the Sea Peoples may all have contributed to the upheavals in Canaan at the beginning of the Iron Age. The entire explanation is not known, but Egyptian power did decline and there was a transition period during which no one group controlled the land of Canaan.

Another part of the question of the origin of the Israelites is the interrelationships of the various peoples who were living in Canaan at the time Egyptian control ended. The Book of Judges gives the impression that three distinct groups fought for control of the land of Canaan at that time: the Canaanites, the Israelites and the Philistines. How accurate is that picture? As we have seen, among the Canaanites there is much imprecision about who they were and how they were related to other peoples. Geographically, no precise boundaries can be drawn, but it is clear that Canaan refers to the land that later became Israel, as well as regions further north. There was no cohesive group of people with an awareness of a common identity as Canaanites; yet there was a similarity of material culture and religion across Canaan. The conventional way of describing the Canaanites is that they were that mix of people living in and around Israel before Israel began, many of whom continued living there after Israel came to be. That description is adequate for our purposes, as long as we keep in mind that these people would not necessarily have considered themselves Canaanites. The question that recent explanations of the origin of the Israelites try to answer is: What was the relationship of the Israelites to that mix of people we call Canaanites?

The Philistines and other Sea Peoples were more identifiable as separate political entities, especially the well-known Philistine league of five cities, but even here there was some blurring of boundaries. Not only did their material culture eventually become the same as their neighbors', but the Old Testament, in Judges and 1 Samuel, speaks of villages going back and forth between Israelite and Philistine rule. Even David joined forces with the Philistines for a time, when Saul was trying to kill him (1 Sm 27). If the Old Testament, which as a rule emphasizes the differences between the Israelites and the Philistines, acknowledges this mixing, then historically there likely was some mixing.

More intriguing is the possibility that other Sea Peoples became part of the Israelites. Trude and Moshe Dothan discuss evidence, suggested earlier by Yigael Yadin, that the tribe of Dan came from the Denyen (or Danuna), one of the peoples mentioned in the Egyptian lists of the Sea Peoples. According to the Old Testament, when the Israelites took possession of the land of Canaan, Dan was allotted a territory along the Mediterranean coast next to what became the Philistines' territory, but the tribe was forced out and finally found a place in northern Galilee (Jos 19:40–48; Jgs 18). Judges 5, an ancient victory song, chastises Dan for not joining the other tribes in a battle against the Canaanites: "And Dan, why did he abide with the ships?" (Jgs 5:17). A possible inference is that some of the Denyen, remembered as a seafaring people, settled on the coast along with the Philistines but later were forced out in a conflict with them and eventually joined with the newly emerging Israelites as the tribe of Dan.[12]

There are stories in the Bible that may support the claim that Dan came from the Sea Peoples. Samson, from the tribe of Dan, married a Philistine woman and was involved with other Philistine women. His subsequent conflicts with the Philistines are not portrayed as part of a larger war between the Israelites and the Philistines, but as a personal matter between him and Philistines (Jgs 13–16). It is possible that the present form of the story of Samson is based on an earlier legend from Sea Peoples who became part of the Israelites.[13] Also, during the monarchy, when the northern tribes broke away and formed a separate kingdom, the Old Testament relates that Jeroboam, their first king, built two national temples, one in Bethel and one in the city of Dan (1 Kgs 12:25–33). It may be that the Danites still had distinct religious traditions that Jeroboam needed to acknowledge by having a separate national temple there. The Book of Amos condemns those who say, "As your god lives, O Dan," as if a different god is worshiped there (Am 8:14). Unfortunately, Amos neglects to tell us the name of the god of Dan.

Archaeological evidence may also support the view that Dan came from the Sea Peoples and spent time near the Philistines and southern early Israelites before migrating to its final northern location. In a survey of the archaeology of Upper Galilee, Rafael Frankel notes that, in general, the pottery of Upper Galilee is different from the collared-rim forms used further south in Samaria and Judah (discussed above in chapter 2). However, at Tel Dan, there was a mixture of Upper Galilee forms, collared-rim forms and Philistine forms.[14] The inhabitants of Dan fit the profile of a migrating group influenced by different peoples, and part of that influence reflects the culture of one of the Sea Peoples, the Philistines.

The relationship of the Canaanites, Philistines and Israelites was more complex than the Book of Judges would lead us to believe. There were many groups present during the upheavals at the beginning of the Iron Age, and the people who became the Israelites probably included a mix of all of them. We should not look for one single origin of the Israelites but for multiple origins. It is difficult to determine when these people of different origins became a single people. Making it even more difficult is the fact that the definition of *Israel* was not static. At the time of the Merneptah Stele the term refers to a small group within Canaan. The Bible uses it to refer to a good-size kingdom at the time of David and Solomon, and after Solomon, to the northern half of that kingdom. During all of that time parts of the land were changing hands among Israel, Philistia, Edom, Moab and other small nations in the region. Most of the Hebrew Scriptures were written after a nation called Israel ceased to exist. It is also necessary to keep in mind Lemche's caution that nationality and ethnicity did not mean the same thing to people in biblical times as it does to people today. Understanding who the Israelites were means understanding them from the vantage point of a constantly shifting identity.

5
Migration and Infiltration

Introduction

This chapter and the two that follow will survey the most recent positions on the origin of the Israelites. These recent positions make use of the increase in archaeological and textual data that have become available since the earlier three classic models were formulated. These views are diverse because there is no consensus on the issue. They do, however, share a common awareness that the investigative process is a complex one and that any rational explanation of the origins of the *majority* of the first Israelites must deal with rather than account for the identity of every person who eventually became an Israelite.

There is no neat way to categorize the various positions of scholars today. Some are revisions of older models; some are new explanations; some try to answer more questions than others. The following three chapters follow an order that first addresses the explanations by those who see a weak connection between the Israelites and the Canaanites and continues to those that see a strong connection. In this chapter I will look at the positions of two scholars who say that the first Israelites were not Canaanites, but people who migrated to Canaan from elsewhere or were nomads who infiltrated the land. In chapter 6, I will look at the views of two who say that the first Israelites were not Canaanites, but people who had been living alongside them for centuries and shared some aspects of their material culture. In chapter 7, I will look at the views of several who say the first Israelites were, in fact, Canaanites. It is a useful arrangement because the major areas of disagreement have to do with the relationship between Israelites and Canaanites. As mentioned at the end of chapter 2, regarding the other major issue that divided scholars in the past— whether the process was violent or peaceful—there is now a basic agreement that it was mainly a peaceful one and that the occasional battles now known to us were not from a single cause.

This arrangement does not imply that there is complete agreement among the scholars that I have grouped together in the same chapter, and likewise there are many points of agreement among positions that I have relegated to different chapters. Because nearly everyone acknowledges that the first Israelites were a mixed people, scholars recognize some element of truth in the views of those they disagree with.

The scholars discussed in these three chapters come from different areas of specialty—Egyptian history, the Hebrew Scriptures, and archaeology of the ancient Near East. Some make use of sociology and anthropology more than others. It is a dilemma common to the study of this issue. It is necessary to pay some attention to all of these fields because analyses from all of them can provide insights into Israel's origins. Yet no one can be an expert in all fields. There is the danger of the scripture scholar oversimplifying or misunderstanding data from archaeology, of the archaeologist using sociology incorrectly and so forth. The best corrective for the problem is to have people from different fields actively involved in the issue. Fortunately, the issue of the Israelites' origins has attracted the interest of people from different fields. It is the kind of issue that promotes dialogue among disciplines, a process that generates advantages far beyond simply finding the answer to one question.

The First Israelites Came from Outside Canaan

Donald Redford and Baruch Halpern both see the early Israelites as people who migrated into Canaan from elsewhere, although they disagree on where the majority of these Israelites came *from.* Both of their explanations have much in common with the classic Peaceful Infiltration model in that they see it as a gradual process of immigrants or nomads settling first in the unoccupied hill country and then gradually expanding and having occasional conflicts with the Canaanite cities. Redford and Halpern also try to incorporate recent archaeological data and knowledge of Canaanite society and the Sea Peoples into their views.

Donald Redford

Donald Redford is professor of Near Eastern studies at the University of Toronto. He has published a number of historical studies, particularly on Egypt, as well as a number of books and articles on Scripture. In his book *Egypt, Canaan, and Israel in Ancient Times,* he discusses the origins of Israel within the context of Egyptian history.[1] Redford begins by reviewing positions he disagrees with. He maintains that the biblical accounts of the patriarchs migrating to Egypt and their descendants escaping from slavery there are not supported in any Egyptian sources and that scholars should abandon the attempt to find some historical ground in the patriarchal and Exodus stories. Redford also criticizes past practices in biblical archaeology—and even opposes the use of the term *biblical archaeology*—for only seeking evidence that proves or disproves events in biblical stories rather than looking toward a broader understanding of ancient Near Eastern society. He praises the sociological approach of George Mendenhall and Norman Gottwald for seeking an alternative explanation for Israel's beginnings, but he disagrees with their conclusions because there is no direct evidence for a social revolution, nor was such an event likely in the circumstances of the ancient Near East. He also criticizes others who say the first Israelites were Canaanites but had a gradual and relatively peaceful beginning; Redford says that people leaving Canaanite cities would not find the highlands a safe place because the area was full of gangs of robbers.[2] After rejecting these other answers to the question, he presents his own explanation.

According to Redford, the *shasu,* mostly living south and east of Canaan, had been a longtime threat to the people of Canaan and an annoyance to Egypt. They had a reputation as robbers, seeking out remote areas and pursuing a lifestyle that seemed uncivilized to the Egyptians. They were a significant component of the population around Canaan during the Late Bronze Age, sometimes representing more than one-third of the list of captives of Egyptian kings. But as Egyptian power declined, the *shasu* began to encroach more into Canaan.[3]

Redford believes that the Israel mentioned on the Merneptah Stele (just before 1200 B.C.E.) could have been a *shasu* enclave; in fact, their presence in Canaan forced Egypt to increase its military presence in an attempt to try to stop their expansion.[4] In the end, Egyptian efforts were not successful, and after 1200 B.C.E. these *shasu* began to develop more villages in the highlands of Canaan, where the Egyptian army and the Canaanite cities were unable or unwilling to exert political control over them.

Redford acknowledges that archaeological evidence shows some similarities in the material cultures of the Canaanites and the early Israelites, but he explains these likenesses by saying that the very earliest settlements in the highlands would have left behind very little archaeological evidence because their ways would still have been similar to the nomadic lifestyle they had just abandoned. Therefore, most of our evidence dates from the time period after they had lived in Canaan long enough to be influenced by Canaanite traditions; since the nomadic *shasu* did not have any architectural tradition of their own, they adopted the house types of the Canaanite lowlands and cities and, eventually, other aspects of their material culture.[5]

These new Israelite settlers were a people distinct from the Canaanites not only in their lifestyle, but also in their religion. Redford says that they did not worship the usual Canaanite gods but worshiped a god, Yahweh, who had been worshiped for centuries by some *shasu*. In some Egyptian lists of *shasu* groups, a place "Yhw in the land of the Shasu" is mentioned, indicating that one of the places they lived was named after the god Yahweh.[6] Their other religious practices were also different from the Canaanite traditions. They located their shrines outside their villages and often had a single shrine serving several nearby villages.[7] The religious organization of the early Israelites, reflected in the Pentateuch as well as in Joshua and Judges, is similar to what would be found in a clan-based nomadic society. There was a belief in a contract with their deity (the covenant referred to in the Pentateuch), leaders were chosen on an ad hoc basis in times of military crisis (the judges) and religious callings were tied up with military leadership (the Nazirite vow of Samson).[8]

Redford's approach attempts to explain how recent archaeological discoveries can be compatible with the Infiltration model. Approaching the issue from the point of view of Egyptian history has value because Egypt was ruling the land of Canaan at the time of Israel's beginnings and because the Old Testament refers to the Israelites' ancestors living in Egypt. However, the claim that the similarities in material culture came about because the new settlers quickly adopted elements of Canaanite material culture is not accepted by most who specialize in the archaeology of Palestine. These dissenters think it more likely that there was a close relationship with the Canaanites before Israel emerged. Also, it is difficult to estimate the number of *shasu* who lived at the time Israel began, and the likelihood that they would settle in villages is uncertain. It may be true that some of the *shasu*, including some who worshiped Yahweh, did become part of Israel, but most scholars believe it unlikely that the majority of the early Israelites had been *shasu*. William Dever and Gösta Ahlström, for example, argue that the beginnings of Israel should be seen mainly as a process that took place within Canaanite society.[9] Redford's explanation could also be criticized for his use of the Bible. On the one hand, he rejects approaches that are too influenced by the biblical story, saying the Old Testament is too late to be of historical value, but on some points, like the organization of society and religion in the Book of Judges, he uses the Bible to support his position. He does not attempt to determine systematically what parts of Judges might be more historical than others; he simply lists all the elements that support his position and then acknowledges that there is some historical uncertainty.

Redford's approach illustrates the need to study this issue from the point of view of different fields. Coming at it from the point of view of Egyptian history provides insights others may not have thought of, and he is able to incorporate data from archaeology and scripture scholarship into a single thesis, although others may criticize particular points in his use of the data.

Baruch Halpern

Baruch Halpern, professor of ancient history and Jewish studies at Pennsylvania State University, has written several books and articles on Israelite history and archaeology, as well as other topics in the field of scripture. His major study on the origin of Israel is *The Emergence of Israel in Canaan,* published in 1983. He also authored the *Anchor Bible Dictionary* article, "Settlement of Canaan."[10] Like Redford, Halpern sees the first Israelites as people who migrated in from the outside. But instead of looking to the *shasu* of the southeast, Halpern looks to Syrians migrating down from the north, and his explanation takes more seriously the literary evidence of the Bible along with the available archaeological evidence.

Halpern rejects the Social Revolution model or other explanations that see the emergence of Israel as mainly a process within Canaanite society. There is no evidence of any flight or migration from the cities to the hill country. In fact, in a time of disruption of the social and economic system, people would be more likely to go to the cities, where there were supplies of grain. Nor is it necessary to posit a social revolution to explain the decentralized and anti-monarchic ideology of early Israel. Those views would develop naturally for people living in the hill country.[11]

Halpern also disagrees with those who use archaeological evidence to say that the early Israelites were Canaanites. The archaeological evidence, he says, is too ambiguous to prove that there was continuity between the material culture of the Canaanites and that of the Israelites. Although they have some characteristics in common, the house types and the pottery have enough differences that it is possible they were made by a group ethnically distinct from the Canaanites but who adopted some Canaanite customs.[12]

Halpern maintains that the archaeological evidence by itself may be ambiguous, but that taken together with the textual evidence, it can only mean that the Israelites came from outside of Canaan.[13] He claims that there is some historical basis to the Book of Joshua's picture of the Hebrews invading Canaan from the east. During the thirteenth century B.C.E., there were waves of migrants coming south from Syria into Transjordan, caused in part by threats of Assyrian expansion.[14] Some of these migrants formed the nations of Ammon, Moab and Edom. Others joined with an Exodus group coming up from Egypt. The Exodus group had become Yahweh worshipers during their migration through Edom, where Yahweh was already worshiped by some desert people. The migrants from the north formed an alliance with the Exodus group and migrated into Canaan from the east.[15]

Once in Canaan this new alliance joined with the Canaanite hill population, already known as Israel (the Israel mentioned on the Merneptah Stele). This unity was aided by the assimilation of their gods—the Yahweh of the new immigrants was equated with the god El of Israel. Halpern sees Shechem as an early cultic center for the new religious alliance and believes that there is some historical basis to the story of the acceptance of the covenant at Shechem in Joshua 24.[16]

Archaeological evidence does indicate that the nations on the other side of the Jordan—Ammon, Moab and Edom—did emerge around the same time that Israel did. Also, the Old Testament portrays those nations as closely related to Israel; the nation of Edom is mentioned as the source of the descendants of Esau, the brother of Jacob (Gn 36), and the nations of Ammon and Moab are named as the sources of the descendants of Lot, Abraham's nephew (Gn 19:30–38). The Old Testament also depicts Abraham as coming to the promised land from Haran in the north, possibly reflecting old memories of migrations from Syria, and it is consistent in portraying the Israelites as a people distinct from the Canaanites, even in passages generally acknowledged to be quite early, such as Exodus 15 (the victory song at the sea) and Judges 5 (Deborah's victory song).[17]

Halpern's explanation has some valuable points. His criticism of the Social Revolution model is shared by many scholars; why posit a revolution for which there is no direct evidence, especially when the results of that revolution can be explained more simply by circumstances known to be true? His attempt to take parts of the biblical story seriously is also refreshing; Halpern avoids the tendency of some to dismiss the whole biblical story if some parts of it are not historical. His explanation also connects the beginning of Israel to the beginnings of the neighboring states of Ammon, Moab and Edom, which accounts for the Old Testament placing their inhabitants as close relatives of the Israelites.

The difficulties with Halpern's explanation are similar to the difficulties with Redford's. We do not know how many of these migrating groups there were and whether it is reasonable to believe that they could account for the majority of the people who became Israelites. Also, as concluded in chapter 2, there is very strong evidence of continuity between the Canaanite and Israelite material cultures, which is hard to explain if most of the Israelites migrated there from elsewhere. Halpern's explanation is valuable inasmuch as it accounts for the roots of some of the early Israelites and for pointing out the weaknesses of some other theories, but most believe it is not the best model for the origin of the majority of the Israelites.

The majority of scholars have abandoned the attempt to treat the early Israelites as outsiders who came to Canaan from elsewhere, whether from the desert of the southeast or from Syria in the north. There is too much similarity between the material culture and religion of the first Israelites and the Canaanites. Nonetheless, there is the fact that the Old Testament, even in early passages, insists that the Israelites are a distinct group, and the fact that worship of Yahweh is not known to have existed in Canaan before the emergence of the Israelites. Any explanation has to account for those facts, at least to say that some of the Israelites might have come from the *shasu* and from Syria and that their stories somehow became central to the identity of the whole nation.

6
Symbiosis

Most scholars today do see some early relationship between the first Israelites and the Canaanites, which accounts for the similarities in material culture and religion. The closeness of that relationship and the nature of the society that ultimately became the Israelites are matters for debate. In this chapter, I will look at the views of two archaeologists who argue for a position *between* those who say that the Israelites were a distinct group who migrated to Canaan from elsewhere (Redford and Halpern) and those who say that the Israelites should be seen as Canaanites (discussed in the next chapter). These two, Volkmar Fritz and Israel Finkelstein, say that the Israelites were not complete outsiders to Canaan but had some previous contact with the Canaanites. Still, they see the ancestors of the Israelites as a distinct group, with their own history, traditions and self-understanding separate from the Canaanites.

Volkmar Fritz

Volkmar Fritz is a German Old-Testament scholar and archaeologist. In analyzing the issue of the origin of the Israelites, he rejects most of the tenets held by the three classic models because they do not adequately account for the available archaeological evidence. He has, however, developed a modified version

of the Infiltration model, which he calls a "Symbiosis hypothe-
sis."[1] Fritz acknowledges that the archaeological evidence paints a
mixed picture—that there are both similarities and differences
between Canaanite and Israelite material culture. He explains this
by maintaining that the first Israelites did not live on the extreme
fringes of the Canaanite lands like the desert bedouins but were
nomads who lived for a long time in close contact with the
Canaanites and thus had adopted some of the Canaanite material
culture before settling down in the new villages of the highlands.

Fritz examines the evidence gathered from large Canaanite
cities and, like others, concludes that the destruction that did occur
was not from a single cause but was spread out over at least fifty
years, from 1200 to 1150 B.C.E. In Gezer, the one city where the
cause of destruction can be determined for certain, Fritz points to
the archaeological evidence as indicating that it was destroyed by
an Egyptian pharaoh.[2] He also looks at the evidence from the new
settlements in the highlands and finds a lack of uniformity: they
varied in size, some were abandoned after a brief period of occupation, and only a few became walled cities. He does find evidence of
a common architecture in the four-room, or broad-room, house, but
he maintains that this style is too different from that of the Canaanite city houses to have developed from them. With reasoning based
on this architectural difference, he concludes that these new settlers
could not have been former inhabitants of the cities but, more
likely, were people unrelated to the Canaanites.[3]

Because there are similarities in other aspects of both material
cultures, especially pottery, Fritz holds that these new settlers must
have been people who had close contact with the Canaanites over a
long period of time. In fact, an *ostracon* (a piece of pottery with
writing on it) from a new settlement at Izbet Sarta uses the proto-
Canaanite alphabet, indicating similarities in language.[4] These
people were the Israelite tribes, living in a symbiotic relationship
with the Canaanites. These Israelites were nomads, but they were
partly sedentary and had developed close economic relationships
with the Canaanites. As the Canaanite cities declined, there was

less advantage to this close relationship, so the Israelites began to establish their own more self-sufficient villages in the highlands, independent of any economic relationship with the Canaanite cities.[5]

Fritz says that the Merneptah Stele, the earliest written mention of Israel, supports this view. On the monument, *Israel* is written with the sign for a people, not a city, thereby inferring that the Israelites were recognized by others as a tribal society, distinct from the people living in the Canaanite cities. Also, the early victory song in Judges 5 fits this picture. It indicates that there was a period when tribal cooperation was not completely established and points to a time of peaceful coexistence between the new Israelites and the Canaanite cities, despite occasional battles.[6]

This explanation is a possible way to combine some of the insights of the earlier Peaceful Infiltration model with recent archaeological evidence. It accounts for the mixed picture portrayed through the archaeological evidence by asserting that the Israelites had close contact with, but were not identical to, the Canaanites. This stance can be criticized, though, for pushing the material differences too far; Fritz maintains that the dissimilarities imply that the early Israelites were unrelated to the Canaanites. But, as Gloria London argues, the variations can be accounted for by the different demands of rural and urban living; she also maintains that the similarities in material culture, including the house types, are too close to allow us to view the first Israelites as unrelated to the Canaanites.[7] Thus, the same archaeological evidence is open to different interpretations. Additional data or more-sophisticated means of analyzing the data will be needed to resolve the debate.

Israel Finkelstein

Israel Finkelstein is an Israeli archaeologist at Tel Aviv University who has studied the issue of the origin of the Israelites in some detail. His 1988 book, *The Archaeology of the Israelite Settlement,* brought together archaeological evidence and his own conclusions on what that evidence says about the origin of the Israelites.[8] In several articles and books since, then he has added additional arguments for his view.

Finkelstein's main thesis is that the emergence of Israel in Iron Age I has to be understood as part of a cyclic process. For centuries, there were periods of expansion of settlements in the hill country of Canaan, followed by periods of decline. Instead of seeing the beginning of Israel as a one-time, unique event, we should relate it to similar settlement expansions of previous periods. Also, like Fritz, Finkelstein looks to nomadic people living in close contact with the Canaanites as the ancestors of the Israelites.

Finkelstein says the material culture does not show that the first Israelites were identical to the Canaanites living in the lowlands. Regarding the architecture, he maintains that the four-room house, with its broad room at the back, had some basis in nomads' tents but really should be seen as a new development in the hill country, based on the huge numbers of people in the new settlements.[9] Although other archaeologists claim it has similarities to Canaanite houses, he points to only one exact parallel from a Canaanite site.[10]

He says that the collared-rim jars, found mainly in Israelite settlements, are found in a few Canaanite sites as well as other places, but these findings are not enough to indicate that the Israelite settlers were Canaanites. More significant is the fact that the pottery of the new settlements has some similarity to that of earlier hill country settlements from Middle Bronze Age II B–C (ca. 1800–1550 B.C.E.), which fits his view that the Israelite settlements should be related to earlier settlements in the hill country.[11]

Finkelstein describes a pastoral or nomadic background for the settlers. He believes there is good evidence that nomads settle down in villages when economic, political or social reasons make it beneficial to do so and that it is not unusual for a whole group of people to go back and forth from a settled to a nomadic way of life over a long period of time.[12] A long tradition of living either in small highland villages or as nomads sets these people apart from those living within the urban culture of the Canaanite cities, although the two groups may have had a close economic relationship with each other at times.

Finkelstein also looks at faunal remains—bones of animals used in their diet—for evidence of who the settlers in the highlands were. He points out that pig bones are found in Iron Age I in sites from the Canaanite lowlands, at Philistine sites and at a site in Ammon on the other side of the Jordan but are absent from the new settlements in the highlands of Canaan. Food is to a large extent determined by environmental and economic factors but is also an important social and religious symbol. Therefore, evidence of a difference in diet could support the claim that the people in the new settlements were a group distinct from the people in the Canaanite cities and others in the region.[13]

To show that the settlement of the highlands in Iron Age I was not a unique event, Finkelstein compares the archaeological data from the Iron I settlements to two earlier increases in settlements in the highlands. These two earlier increases, the first in the Early Bronze Age I (3300–3050 B.C.E.) and the second in Middle Bronze II B–C (1800–1550 B.C.E.), had the following similarities to the increase in Iron Age I: In all three periods, the majority of the settlements were unfortified; there was a preference for settling in the same locales; the society included a mix of sedentary and pastoral people; the pottery was utilitarian and luxury items were rare; and the outcome was similar—the development of the Israelite state resembled the formation of territorial states in the Middle and Late Bronze Ages and perhaps also the Early Bronze Age. Finkelstein also finds similarities in the periods of decline between the eras of increased settlement.[14] Therefore, the Iron I settlements should be seen as one phase of a cyclic phenomenon in the hill country of Canaan.

Finkelstein's conclusion is that there was a group distinct from the Canaanites and others in the region, who went back and forth from a sedentary to a pastoralist/nomadic lifestyle. These people did not become nomads in the sense of dwelling in the deep desert but remained close to the Canaanite hill country and, along with those still living in villages, were part of a dimorphic society.[15] Because of their contact with Canaanite society, they were already familiar with Canaanite material culture and quickly adopted aspects of it when they settled down in villages. This was a peaceful process, but as the settlements increased and the new-comers needed more land, there began to be conflicts with the Canaanite cities.[16]

Finkelstein's explanation is valuable for the broad archaeological expertise he brings to the subject. His attention to other evidence besides pottery and architecture gives him a firmer basis to discuss ethnicity and distinctions between groups. It is also a valuable approach in that he puts the issue in a larger time frame than most others do. Like Fritz, he attempts to account for the mixed archaeological picture—he views the new settlements as having some similarities to the Canaanites in their material culture but some differences as well, and, like Fritz, he explains the situation by saying that the new settlers were a distinct group of people but lived in close contact with the Canaanites.

Criticism of Finkelstein's view comes from other archaeologists who make more of the similarities in material culture. The similarities in pottery, religious items and house types are numerous, and if most of the differences can be explained by the different demands of rural highland living, it makes sense to many to see the first Israelites as ethnically identical to the Canaanites. Also, there is the possibility that he pushes the parallels with the earlier periods of settlement in the hill country too far. Finkelstein acknowledges that the beginnings of Israel must be seen as a "combination of long-term history and short-term circumstances and by a balance between local developments and external influences."[17] However, he puts more emphasis on long-term history and local developments and could be accused of not giving enough attention to unique, short-term circumstances that affected the beginning of Israel. Finally, those who see some historical truth in the biblical record will disagree with Finkelstein's dismissal of it. He refers to it as "irrelevant" and believes that those who see the beginning of Israel as a unique event are clinging too closely to a biblical view.[18]

Both Fritz and Finkelstein treat the ancestors of the Israelites as ethnically distinct from the Canaanites. That is a difficult issue to evaluate because it is not always clear what constitutes an ethnic group and because Fritz and Finkelstein speak of a complex, shifting relationship with the Canaanites. The view of Donald Redford and Baruch Halpern, discussed in the last chapter, was that Israel came to Canaan from elsewhere. If that is correct, then obviously the Israelites should be considered ethnically distinct from the Canaanites. The views discussed in the next chapter go to the opposite extreme, taking the position that the Israelites' ancestors should be considered identical to the Canaanites. Because Fritz and Finkelstein fall somewhere in between, it is necessary to be clear on what their understanding of ethnicity is. According to Finkelstein, an ethnic group is defined by a combination of self-ascribed factors as well as factors attributed to the group by others. These factors include a common ancestry (real or fictitious), common customs, language, religion, values, morality and etiquette. The difficulty is that much of what constitutes ethnicity involves untraceable social networks rather than the material remains we can gather from archaeology.[19]

As we will see in the next chapter, William Dever also takes up the issue of ethnicity, coming to a conclusion that differs from Finkelstein's. Then there is Niels Lemche's caution that any use of the term *ethnicity* is misleading. Ethnic boundaries are not static, and a person could conceivably have more than one ethnic identity at the same time. It is not always clear how to categorize ethnic groups today, and it is even more difficult to do so with ancient peoples who are not completely known to us. This is an issue that needs further input from sociologists and anthropologists, and we need to ask if the notion of ethnicity is a useful one in discussing the origin of the Israelites.

7
The First Israelites Were Canaanites

All of the views discussed in this chapter claim that the first Israelites were indigenous to Canaan, but beyond that, they are more diverse than the views grouped together in the last two chapters. The differences among these five scholars have to do with the more speculative aspects of each scholar's views. Regarding the identity of the Israelites' ancestors—an issue about which we have a goodly amount of concrete evidence—there is basic agreement among these scholars that they were Canaanites (although Robert Coote also sees the *shasu* as having an important role). Because more scholarly positions are discussed in this chapter than in the previous two, and also in view of the diversity of these positions, I have divided the chapter into three parts. The first will focus on the views of William Dever, Niels Peter Lemche and Gösta Ahlström, who describe a complex resettlement of Canaanites from the cities and rural areas into the new settlements of the highlands. Next will be an updating of Norman Gottwald's Social Revolution model. Last, we will discuss Robert Coote's theory that Egypt used Israel as its agent in controlling Palestine.

A. Canaanite Resettlement

William Dever

William Dever is an American archaeologist who bases his conclusions mainly on data in his field, although he is also careful to indicate segments of the biblical story that are either compatible or incompatible with the archaeological evidence. Using that evidence, especially the lack of destruction of Canaanite cities, he maintains that the Conquest model should be ruled out.[1] He also disagrees with the Peaceful Infiltration model because the archaeological evidence does not support it and because the material culture of the new settlements, especially the pottery, shows clear continuity with Canaanite material culture.[2]

With regard to continuity the archaeological evidence may strongly indicate that the ancestors of the Israelites were Canaanites, but it doesn't tell us everything about how they emerged as a people. Dever says:

> The inescapable conclusion—only likely to be enhanced by future archaeological research—is that the Israelite settlement in Canaan was part of the larger transition from the Late Bronze to the Iron Age. It was a gradual, exceedingly complex process, involving social, economic, and political—as well as religious—change, with many regional variations.[3]

Dever says that Gottwald's Social Revolution model is compatible with the archaeological evidence but that it is an artificial construct that cannot be tested archaeologically.[4] Dever expresses some agreement with Volkmar Fritz that many of the early Israelites could have been people who lived near the Canaanites for a long period of time and thus absorbed much of their material culture.[5] But Dever concludes that it is best to see Israel as emerging from various backgrounds, namely, those of urban Canaanites, rural Canaanites, some nomadic people and perhaps a small number of escaped slaves from Egypt. For the most part, the emergence of the Israelites should be seen as part of a transformation within Canaanite society, not as a change caused by new people migrating in.[6]

In discussing Israel's emergence, Dever takes up the difficult issue of ethnicity. His definition of an ethnic group includes the following characteristics: it is biologically self-perpetuating; its members share a fundamental, recognizable, uniform set of cultural values, including language; it forms a partly independent interaction sphere; its constituents define themselves, and are defined by others, as a category distinct from other categories of the same order; finally, the group shares some sense of the boundaries of its ethnic unit and acknowledges a set of rules for social interaction with people outside the group.[7] Some parts of this definition may seem vague and impossible to determine from the limited remains we have from ancient Israel, but Dever uses it to test whether the material remains of the new settlements in the highlands in Iron Age I belong to a new ethnic group. His conclusion is that there is enough continuity with the material culture of the Canaanites to support the view that the settlers came from the Canaanites but that their way of life changed significantly enough to indicate the emergence of a new ethnic group distinct from the other Canaanites. The major changes in their way of life included living in scattered small villages rather than in an urban culture; isolation from other people because most of the settlements lack imported items; and a less stratified social structure. Therefore, the ancestors of the Israelites were Canaanites, but early in Iron Age I a new ethnic group emerged from the Canaanites. This new group Dever refers to as the "Proto-Israelites." He prefers to use this name for the Iron Age I settlers rather than "Israelites" because they had not yet developed into the Israel of the Old Testament.[8]

The value of Dever's explanation is the careful interpretation of the archaeological evidence that he brings to the issue. He also reminds us of the limitations of the archaeological evidence. His picture of the emergence of Israel is not characterized by as much speculation as Gottwald's or Coote's; he acknowledges that the more speculative models *could* fit the archaeological evidence, but he prefers to stay with what is more concretely known. When the evidence does indicate something, such as continuity in material culture, then that should be treated as a fact, and any explanation has to account for it. But models that go beyond that and try to explain the process in more detail can only be viewed as consistent with the archaeological evidence and not supported by it. His conclusion that the process was a mixed and complex one that defies full understanding may not be satisfying to those of us looking for a more definitive answer, but it is a needed reminder that we are a long way from that definitive answer.

Dever's thoughts on ethnicity have been strongly criticized by Finkelstein, who sees the Iron Age I Proto-Israelites not as a new ethnic group, but as people who existed for centuries, going back and forth from a sedentary to a more nomadic lifestyle. For Finkelstein, it was only in the emergence of its monarchy that a new ethnic group, the Israelites, can be said to have emerged. Because both Dever and Finkelstein are trying to determine ethnicity on the basis of incomplete remains, it is a hard debate to evaluate. Further work on ethnicity is needed to make it a more precise concept in discussing early Israel or to decide if the notion of ethnicity should be used at all.

Niels Peter Lemche

Niels Peter Lemche, a scripture scholar at the University of Copenhagen in Denmark also sees the beginning of Israel as an internal change within Canaanite society. In *Early Israel: Anthropological and Historical Studies on the Israelite Society Before the Monarchy*[9] and later in *Ancient Israel: A New History of Israelite Society,*[10] he spends time discussing the social and economic situation of Late Bronze Age Canaanites in the cities and on the farmland controlled by the cities. The king was absolute owner of everything; the craftspeople and bureaucrats in the cities

were his slaves; lower-class workers in the city were never completely free, especially because of the taxes owed to the king.[11]

The rural peasants were the most vulnerable people in
Canaanite society. They lived in unfortified villages and were
unable to accumulate wealth because of the taxes owed to the king.
In times of battles between cities or with the Egyptian army and at
any time of upheaval, the rural peasants could try to take refuge in
the cities, where they may or may not have been given refuge; or
they may have fled to the highlands, giving up their farm life but
perhaps finding more security in a highland community.[12]

A number of factors contributed to deteriorating conditions
around the city states. Egyptian power declined. The Sea Peoples
arrived, further weakening Egypt. The cities became fiercer in
their rivalries with each other once Egypt began to lose control
over Canaan. As the cities could no longer provide security for the
peasant farmers but still demanded taxes from them, more and
more peasants left to join the *hapiru,* who were mainly living in
the highlands of north and central Palestine. As the number of
hapiru increased, they settled more villages in the highlands,
developing into a less outlaw-ridden group and into a more struc-
tured agrarian society.[13]

Like Dever, Lemche uses an internal process to explain the
origin of the Israelites because of the archaeological evidence
showing continuity in material culture: Late Bronze Age urban
material culture cannot be distinguished from the material culture
of the new villages in Iron Age I, taking account of different
demands of urban and rural living.[14] Apart from the Sea Peoples
on the coast, there is no direct evidence of waves of immigrants
coming into Canaan.[15] He also sees the new settlements that
became Israel as consisting mainly of the peasant farmers around
the cities, who would have made up about 90 percent of the population of Canaan.[16] These peasants would already be in the habit
of organizing themselves by kinship, thus fostering a structure
that would develop into the tribal relationships of the new
Israelite society. Coming from an agricultural background, these

peasants would already have enough understanding of building terraces and cisterns to establish agricultural villages in the highlands; it would be much less likely for nomadic people to learn such technology so quickly.[17]

Lemche's caution about using the notion of ethnicity to talk about early Israel has already been mentioned in chapter 4. Our ideas of nationality and ethnicity do not correspond to the ways in which ancient people would categorize themselves. Furthermore, the ways in which any given people categorize themselves are often done for ideological or religious reasons and might not correspond to the methods by which other people living at the same time would categorize them. But because of the similarities in material culture and religion, Lemche does say that the Israelites and Canaanites should not be characterized as representing two distinct cultures; both should be referred to as components of the "Western Asiatic peoples."[18]

Lemche does not leave things as "up in the air" as Dever does, but he does take a similar position, namely, that a gradual, internal process, involving only occasional violence, effected the Israelites' development from the roots of Canaanite society.

Gösta Ahlström

Gösta Ahlström is originally from Sweden and came to the United States and the University of Chicago, where he published works on early Israelite history until his death in 1992. He studied the identity of the first Israelites in his 1986 book, *Who Were the Israelites?*[19] More recently, in *The History of Ancient Palestine,* he undertook a more ambitious history, one that extended from prehistoric times to the Persian period.[20] This latter work is perhaps the most useful recent history of Israel. It brings together archaeological data and a critical analysis of texts, both from the Bible and elsewhere. Ahlström rejects the three classic models, maintaining that the first Israelites were mostly Canaanites from the cities and rural lowlands.

Ahlström draws more information from the Merneptah Stele than just the fact that there was some group called Israel by 1200 B.C.E. He points out that the names of the defeated peoples listed on the monument are arranged in a ring structure. The first and last places mentioned are large regions; the next ring inside includes Canaan and Israel, representing smaller territories; at the center of the structure, individual city-states are mentioned— Ashkelon, Gezer and Yeno'am. Canaan and Israel therefore represent the two parts of Palestine. Because the word *Canaan* normally refers to the urban lowlands, then it follows that use of the term *Israel* must be a designation for the hill country. Also, *Israel* is written with the sign for a people rather than a city or nation, meaning that this group of people was seen by Egypt as more loosely organized; anyone from any background who settled in the hill country would be considered part of Israel by the Egyptians.[21] Ahlström also maintains that the military campaign referred to on the Merneptah Stele is the same one depicted on a relief at a temple at Karnak in Egypt, showing the Israelites dressed the same as other Canaanites, indicating they were not people who migrated into Canaan from the outside.[22]

Ahlström also concludes from analyses of the pottery and architecture that Israelite material culture is in continuity with Canaanite material culture. Their cisterns and agricultural terraces were not new inventions but were continued from Canaanite use. The pottery and house types also show continuity with Canaanite forms, although adapted for rural living in the hills.[23] According to Ahlström, an increasing number of Canaanites migrated from the lowlands to the highlands to avoid the battles frequently occurring among the cities and to escape the high taxation imposed on them. As circumstances deteriorated in the cities, there was even more motivation to migrate to the more secure villages. These Canaanite settlers were joined by various refugees and bandits from inside and outside of Canaan.[24] Gradually they developed a common identity as one people.

Ahlström's explanation for the origin of the Israelites is not fundamentally different from Dever's or Lemche's: Canaanites from the cities and lowlands gradually left, for reasons of security and economics, and settled new villages in the highlands. His contribution has, however, brought together a great body of literary and archaeological evidence touching on the issue and has put it in the broader context of Palestinian history.

B. Social Revolution—Norman Gottwald

Norman Gottwald continues to defend and revise his Social Revolution model. A useful source of his views since *The Tribes of Yahweh,* published in 1979, is a collection of essays published in 1993, *The Hebrew Bible in Its Social World and Ours.*[25] He has also written an introduction to the entire Hebrew Bible, *The Hebrew Bible: A Socio-Literary Introduction,*[26] and other books and articles. He expresses agreement with the general picture depicted by Dever, Ahlström and Lemche: that Israel emerged from the indigenous Canaanite society of the thirteenth and twelfth centuries B.C.E.; that the new Israelite society was made up mainly of farmers but probably also included a mix of craftspeople, former bureaucrats from the cities, priests, nomads and others; that they developed a diversified agricultural economy in the highlands; and that this new society was able to control its own surplus (the people were paying no taxes or tribute to anyone else) for two centuries.[27]

For Gottwald, there are two issues at stake. The first is, *who* were the first Israelites? On this issue, he defends the position that they were indigenous to Canaan, using arguments from archaeology similar to the others discussed in this chapter.

The other issue for Gottwald is, *how* did Israel emerge? It is here that he takes a position different from the others in this chapter, claiming that there was an intentional social revolution. The basics of this model have already been discussed in chapter 3 and will not be repeated here. But Gottwald acknowledges that earlier expressions of the theory may have overstated how sudden, cataclysmic and conclusive the revolt was. In fact, revolutionary tendencies had been present for decades in Canaan, but it took a long time for the various groups involved to unify. The urban lower classes, rural peasants, pastoral nomads, *hapiru* and *shasu* did not have traditions of intercooperating and only slowly coalesced into a revolutionary force. The revolt met varying responses from the Canaanite cities—sometimes the urbanites delivered fierce resistance; sometimes converts from a besieged city joined the rebels; sometimes groups and individuals shifted their allegiance back and forth. It was a slow process, marked by victories and defeats, before a new society known as Israel emerged.[28]

Gottwald also prefers terminology different from that which he used in the past. Instead of *peasant revolt,* he prefers the term *social revolution* because he came to view the process as a broader movement that involved other groups in addition to the peasant farmers, one that was much more gradual than a single uprising. Instead of saying that a "feudal society" was replaced by an "egalitarian society," he now prefers to say that a "tributary mode of production" was replaced by a "communitarian mode of production." *Feudal* and *egalitarian* were not entirely precise; the main difference between the Canaanite economic system and the new Israelite system was that the new villages were able to keep their surplus production rather than turn it over to a ruling class in the form of taxes, rent or interest on loans.[29]

In addition to refining the nuances of the model, Gottwald has responded to critics who say that it is too speculative, that there is no concrete evidence to prove it occurred and that the biblical story relates a completely different series of events. As concrete supporting evidence for the model, Gottwald maintains that a major economic and social shift occurred in the highlands of Canaan during Iron Age I. Canaan went from a stratified society with a centralized economic system in which the rich took the produce of the poor, to a less stratified, decentralized system in which the agricultural producers were able to keep their surplus. The outcome was certainly a favorable one for a social revolution, so the question is, did this situation come about by chance? Was it only because of the accident of a power vacuum after the decline of Egypt and the Canaanite cities and before David established his kingdom that the new Israelite villages lived in this way, or did they deliberately pursue these freedoms— keeping their own surplus and living in a decentralized tribal society—by actively hastening the decline of the rule of Egypt and the Canaanite cities and by purposely trying to prevent a monarchy from developing among themselves? If it was a deliberate effort, then some form of social revolution did take place.[30]

Gottwald offers evidence from the Hebrew Scriptures for believing the process to be a deliberate social revolution. Such a course of events would better explain why the tribal period continued for two centuries instead of almost immediately developing into a monarchy. It would explain why kingship was such a disputed issue in the First Book of Samuel (e.g., Samuel's speech in 1 Sm 8). It would also explain the survival of tribal practices, such as keeping land ownership within the clan, into later Israelite history.[31] Gottwald also offers archaeological evidence that such practices represented a deliberate effort to form a self-sufficient society separate from other Canaanites. The grain pits found at the new villages indicate that surpluses were stored in order to avoid economic dependence on other peoples.[32]

Gottwald raises difficult questions. How can one determine whether certain historical events happened because of complex reasons beyond the control of the major characters or whether these events occurred because *of* their ideological beliefs? There is no direct evidence that such a social revolution took place. We know the outcome of the events that transpired between 1200 and 1000 B.C.E. Gottwald's position represents a possible explanation, but scholars must continue to debate regarding whether or not it is the most likely one.

C. Egyptian Agent—Robert Coote

Robert Coote is professor of Old Testament at San Francisco Theological Seminary. In 1987 he coauthored, with Keith Whitelam, *The Emergence of Early Israel in Historical Perspective.*[33] More recently, he has written *Early Israel: A New Horizon.*[34] He agrees with Dever, Lemche, Ahlström and Gottwald in saying that most of the first Israelites were indigenous to Canaan, although he also believes that a significant number of *shasu* were involved. The major difference between him and the others is his explanation of how Israel forged its beginnings and became powerful enough to control Palestine.

Coote begins with the Merneptah Stele, the earliest mention of Israel. He, too, points out that *Israel* is written differently from the other names on the list, indicating it was not a state or territory but a people. Israel must therefore have been a tribal organization, the form of political entity that existed other than the state. Coote discusses in some detail what tribal organizations were: They existed alongside the city-states of Canaan, sometimes in cooperation and sometimes in conflict with the city-states, as an alternative way in which people could organize themselves. The tribal organizations claimed to share a biological lineage but in fact were frequently shifting in alliances; the claimed genealogy was fiction, meant to express degree of obligation between parts of the tribe. Tribal relationships were part of the social organization of all people in Canaan; such group ties existed among people in cities, among rural peasants, among *hapiru* and among nomadic people.[35]

Coote believes that many of the people included in the Israel of the Merneptah Stele could have been *shasu,* or at least considered part of the *shasu* by Egypt, because of their tribal characteristics. He agrees to some extent with Finkelstein and Fritz in saying that *shasu* expanding their territory and settling in villages accounted for part of the origin of Israel. But unlike the scholars who see the ancestors of Israel mainly as nomadic people, he says that the tribal relationships also extended to farmers and villagers in Canaan. The Merneptah Stele suggests a tribal relationship among the people it calls Israel, but this by itself does not give us any details about whether most of the Israelites were from a nomadic or a sedentary background.[36]

Israel, then, around 1200 B.C.E. was a tribal organization in northern Palestine, consisting mostly of small farmers and their families. It was large enough to be mentioned on the Merneptah Stele, suggesting that it was more than one small tribe and probably a coalition of tribes. As the city-states were declining and as Egyptian control was becoming less firm over Canaan, the tribal organizations would become more politically relevant. The importance that Egypt gave to Israel by mentioning it in the list indicates the beginning of its increase in power.

At this point Coote departs from the other scholars discussed in this chapter. He views Egypt as wanting to have the Israelite tribal organization under its control to use as a buffer between itself and the Hittite-controlled territories to the north.[37] Having a tribal coalition to serve Egyptian military purposes became more important as the city-states declined and the Philistines began to expand their territory in Palestine. For that reason, after defeating Israel (the event mentioned in the Merneptah Stele), Egypt began to use Israel as its agent in trying to maintain control of Palestine. The tribal elite of Israel may have been involved in collecting taxes from farmers to turn over to the Egyptians or in supplying local people to work on Egyptian projects. The support Egypt gave to Israel made it possible for Israel to expand and eventually develop into the nation that controlled Palestine. Evidence of a close relationship between the early Israelites and the Egyptians includes the Egyptian names of several Israelite leaders recorded in the Old Testament: Moses, Aaron, Phineas, Hophni and Merari.[38]

The insights of Coote take account of the shifts in power that occurred in the ancient Near East, and he tries to explain how an apparently insignificant Israel could achieve a start and become a nation. His explanation is also valuable for its appreciation of the political role of tribes at the time that Egypt and the Canaanite city-states were ruling and for its clarification of how a tribal coalition could become powerful in times of shifts of power. Furthermore, his explanation is consistent with evidence showing continuity between Israelite and Canaanite material culture and gives a well-founded accounting for the presence of *shasu* and other groups in the region. It is, or course, a speculative explanation that pushes the evidence further than the other explanations. At the present time there is not enough substantiation to prove or disprove it.

One question that Coote's explanation does not answer well is why the Bible tells such a different story. The Old Testament portrays the first Israelites as cruelly treated slaves in Egypt; Coote says that it was thanks to Egyptian support that Israel survived and became powerful. He also claims that the Bible's story is really not so different—that other than the Song of Miriam (Ex 15), the Old Testament is not hostile to Egypt. That claim seems to overlook large parts of the Bible. Coote says that the Exodus story was adopted by David as a favor to tribal allies in the Negev, which is possible but not very convincing.[39]

If there is truth in Coote's idea of Egyptian support for the growth of a Canaanite tribal organization called Israel, it may explain the beginnings of some segments of the Israelite people. But in view of the story that did eventually become the national story of origins, it is more likely that the majority of people who became Israelites were in a less friendly relationship with Egypt than Coote's explanation suggests.

Summary

There are significant differences among the positions discussed in this chapter. They all say that the early Israelites were indigenous to Canaan, but notwithstanding the same archaeological and textual evidence, they come up with vastly different descriptions of the process by which the Israelites became a people.

Despite their differences, these scholars, as well as the ones discussed in the last two chapters, are in agreement that the Israelites
came from multiple backgrounds. Much more than the three classic
models, these recent explanations acknowledge that no one model
is adequate. These explanations highlight different aspects of the
first Israelites. Further research is needed to determine which
explanation best describes who the majority of these Israelites were
and what the principal process was that led to their emergence in
the land of Canaan.

8
Conclusions

Late-Bronze-Age Canaan was a place of mixed population—both urban and rural, with different classes of people in the cities and in the countryside. Taking account of the variations in wealth and the different demands of urban and rural living, across Canaan there existed a similar material culture. There also was much similarity in religion. However, there had never been any political unity or sense of national identity among the people living in Canaan. Thus, the period of disruption at the beginning of Iron Age I, when the stability provided by Egypt came to an end, was a time that could have developed in several different directions.

Some people found stability in new agricultural villages in the highlands. Most of these people, at least at the beginning of this era, would have come from some rural background—peasants under the control of the ruling class in the large cities, or *hapiru* or nomads already nearby, but it is also likely, especially as time went on and the cities continued to decline, that many people from the large cities resettled in these new villages as well.

Other people tried to keep the cities thriving. The people who wanted to maintain the cities were most likely the people who had the most invested there—members of the ruling families, other wealthy people, those skilled in specialized crafts useful only in large cities or priests connected with the urban temples. Because the cities held on for some time, there were some battles between these cities and developing coalitions of the new villages.

Another group, known collectively as the Sea Peoples, arrived in the eastern Mediterranean and tried to settle down. One part of the Sea Peoples, the Philistines, established dominion over part of Canaan. We are used to thinking of the Philistines only as enemies of the Israelites, but because nearly everyone recognizes that the beginnings of Israel was a mixed process, even the Philistines and other Sea Peoples should be considered as potential members of the combination of people that became the Israelites. There is good reason to believe that one part of the Sea Peoples, the Denyen, became part of Israel and formed the tribe of Dan. It should not be surprising if there was some mixing between the Sea Peoples and the newly emerging Israelites because the Bible itself speaks of David joining with the Philistines for a time (1 Sm 27).

In time, the new villages in the highlands and the Philistine settlements began to thrive more than the old Canaanite cities, but it was some time before the villages were politically unified. The early victory song in Judges 5 gives one picture of the degree of cooperation among the tribes of the highlands. The cooperation was not complete and probably would have been less so in times of peace. If the people in different villages came from varying backgrounds and had no history of cooperation, it was to be expected that during the period of the judges there was a lack of unity.

Around 1050–1000 B.C.E. these villages did become unified, and the name *Israel,* which early in Iron Age I had applied to one tribe or a small coalition of tribes, came to apply to all of them. The reasons for that unity could have included a greater need for cooperation to resist the Philistines, a desire for more stability to increase trade and prosperity, or a common effort to lessen the possibility of one group becoming powerful enough to dominate the others. The details of how this decentralized society developed into a state are not completely known and are beyond the scope of this book.[1]

Although there is not a complete consensus, there is a growing belief among scholars that all of this (with the exceptions of the appearance of the Sea Peoples and possibly the arrival of a small Exodus group) should be considered a transition within Canaanite society. The mix of people who settled the new highland villages included peasant farmers formerly associated with the cities, people from the cities themselves, some *hapiru,* some nomadic people near the Canaanite cities and some migrants from farther away. While the proportionate number of each group of people is unknown, it is more reasonable to conclude that the majority were indigenous to Canaan. The similarities in material culture and religion would be fewer if most of these people were from outside of Canaan.

There was most likely regional variation in the mix of peoples. In the Negev and southern Judah the *shasu* or seminomadic people living closer to the Canaanites may have made up a significant percentage of the people who became Israelites. Further north, a combination of *hapiru* and people from the Canaanite cites and farms probably made up the majority of the ancestors of the Israelites. Then there were groups migrating into the land, such as the tribe of Dan and perhaps groups from Syria and elsewhere, who settled wherever they were finally able to find a place.

Most scholars do not yet see any compelling reason to accept the idea that an ideological social revolution took place. The geography of the highlands themselves would have imposed a more decentralized social order. Dislike of city kings would have come naturally to the rural people, even if no organized revolt had taken place. The cities were in a state of decay for several reasons and would have continued their downward spiral even without a social revolution to hasten their decline. There is no evidence to rule out a social revolution, so it is possible that future discoveries of texts or other evidence would force us to look at that model more seriously. But at the present time there are no direct indications that such an intentional revolution took place.

Similarly, the speculative model proposed by Robert Coote needs more direct evidence to support it. It is a possible explanation, but the same outcome can be explained in other ways more closely related to the concrete evidence.

The most likely process responsible for the emergence of the Israelites was a gradual Canaanite Resettlement similar to the views of William Dever, Niels Peter Lemche and Gösta Ahlström. The decline of the city-states caused an increase in the number of people who found the highlands a better place to live. For some, it was more secure because the cities and the Egyptian army had become less adept at maintaining stability in the plains area. For some, it was an escape from economic hardship because they desired to break away from debt or taxation in the cities. As the strength and unity of the new Israelites increased, others would have joined them rather than continue to resist. This resettlement was by no means a sudden flight from the cities to the countryside; it was a gradual process, from about 1200 to 1050 B.C.E.

There are two additional questions that have important theological interest, although there is little direct evidence to answer them. The first involves the role of the Exodus saga in this process, as well as how it became the national story of all of Israel. If an Exodus group did exist, it must have been small. The transitions taking place in Canaan at that time, along with the mix of population groups already settled there, might have provided a setting conducive for the migration and settling of yet another group in the highlands of Canaan. How did the elaborate and theologically shaped story of that group become everyone's story? Perhaps other people found the idea of escape from Egyptian oppression appealing because the one thing that most of them had in common was some former experience under Egyptian rule. Perhaps the descendants of the Exodus band came to comprise the majority of the dominant group and made their story the national story. At this point there is not enough evidence to answer the question definitively.

The other topic involves the origin of the worship of Yahweh. This is a much broader issue than the present work can deal with, but because it is related to the origin of the Israelites, a few thoughts are in order. By the time the Old Testament was written, Yahweh had become the chief god for Israel, but that was not true at the beginning. The name *Israel* itself indicates that the people who first bore that collective name (although not necessarily the majority of the people who eventually became Israelites) considered the Canaanite god El their chief god. There is no indication of a Canaanite god named Yahweh in the Ugaritic religious epics, but of course our knowledge of Canaanite religion is still limited. The discovery of additional texts could prove worship of Yahweh in pre-Israelite Canaan.

It is often suggested that worship of Yahweh came from Edom or somewhere else in the south. There is possible evidence that *shasu* in the region of Edom worshiped Yahweh,[2] although that evidence is disputed.[3] The early Hebrew poetry discussed in chapter 3 may also indicate early traditions of Yahweh coming from the south: "Yahweh comes from Sinai, He rises from Seir for them, and shines from Mount Paran" (Dt 33:2); "Yahweh, when you went out from Seir, when you marched from the land of Edom..." (Jgs 5:4); "God came from Teman, the Holy One from Mount Paran" (Hb 3:3). The evidence is suggestive, but it is not substantial enough to say with certainty where the worship of Yahweh came from. If the Exodus group became Yahweh worshipers before settling in Canaan, then whatever led to their saga becoming the national story would also explain how Yahweh became the national god of Israel.

Future Research

At this point there is no consensus on the issue of the origin of the Israelites, but more research may help to clarify some matters. Those interested in the topic have benefited in recent years from the fresh views of archaeologists, biblical scholars and historians who have suggested new models or given us reasons to look again at older models. Some have been cautious about reading too much into the evidence; some have developed more imaginative models that go far beyond the evidence. All of the views discussed in this book are valuable in that they stimulate us to think about this question from new angles.

Research on this topic would be helped by a better understanding of Canaanite demographics. A more comprehensive grasp of the total population makeup in Canaan, including the proportion who lived in cities, worked as peasant farmers, served in the military, worked as slaves, belonged to the *hapiru* or were anything else, would help us understand how dramatic a change it would have been for any of them to settle in new villages in the highlands. Even though the large Canaanite cities were so different from the small villages in the hills, perhaps for the majority of the Canaanites it would not have been such a drastic change in lifestyle.

Related to a better understanding of Canaanite demographics is the need for continued dialogue with sociologists and anthropologists on all questions concerning early Israel. The study of the origin of the Israelites does not belong to one single field, and it is impossible for anyone to be an expert in scripture, anthropology, sociology, archaeology and the natural sciences that assist archaeology. Gone are the days of W. F. Albright, when one could be enough of an all-around expert to take on the whole issue. If the issue continues to attract the interest of people from different fields, that dialogue will be fostered. Of course, anyone who attempts to incorporate insights from other fields makes him- or herself vulnerable to criticism for not using the data correctly; that risk is necessary if we are to come closer to an answering to this question.

Research on this topic would also be helped by more knowledge of climatic changes in the ancient Near East. Ze'ev Herzog has suggested that climate change rather than political change was the major factor in the establishment of the Israelite settlements.[4] Information on past history of climate changes and how they affected the population of Canaan would be of great help. The changes that occurred at the end of the Late Bronze Age may have been affected by environmental factors that we have not looked at closely enough.

Views on this topic, of course, could change dramatically with the discovery of new texts. We depend heavily on the Amarna letters, but they are limited to one time period that is slightly earlier than the one we are interested in. The Ugaritic religious epics are also valuable, but they are also slightly removed in time and distance from the beginnings of Israel. The Bible directly addresses the issue of Israelite origins but is even more removed in time than the other sources and has a theological purpose that limits its value as a historical source. Archives of letters or other records from the Canaanite kings of the twelfth century B.C.E. must have existed; the discovery of such material would be invaluable.

In the meantime, the evidence we have is open to various interpretations. The question of the origin of the Israelites is far from being answered.

Notes

Chapter One: The Issue

1. J. Pritchard, ed., *Ancient Near Eastern Texts Relating to the Old Testament,* 3rd edition (Princeton: Princeton University Press, 1969), 219–20.

2. See R. Hendel, "Finding Historical Memories in the Patriarchal Narratives," *Biblical Archaeology Review* 21 (July/Aug. 1995): 52–59, 70–71. For a view that claims more historicity, see K. Kitchen, "The Patriarchal Age: Myth or History?" *Biblical Archaeology Review* 21 (Mar./Apr. 1995): 48–57, 88–95.

3. A. Mazar, *Archaeology of the Land of the Bible: 10,000–586 B.C.E.* (New York: Doubleday, 1990), 328–34.

4. "The Joseph and Moses Narratives," in *Israelite and Judaean History,* ed. by J. Hayes and J. M. Miller (Philadelphia: Trinity Press International, 1977), 212.

5. *The Tribes of Yahweh: A Sociology of the Religion of Liberated Israel, 1250–1050 B.C.E.* (Maryknoll: Orbis Books, 1979), 451–53.

6. 3rd ed. (Philadelphia: Westminster Press, 1981), 120–43.

7. B. Halpern, "The Exodus from Egypt: Myth or Reality?" in H. Shanks, ed. *The Rise of Ancient Israel* (Washington: Biblical Archaeology Society, 1992), 87–113. A description of the pursuit of runaway slaves in Egypt can be found in *Ancient Near Eastern Texts Relating to the Old Testament,* 259.

8. *Ancient Israel: A New History of Israelite Society* (Sheffield, England: JSOT Press, 1988), 75–88.

9. *Joshua,* Anchor Bible (New York: Doubleday, 1982) 27–37, 216–30.

10. *Studies in Ancient Yahwistic Poetry* (Missoula, Mont.: Scholars Press, 1975). See also A. Saenz-Badillos, *A History of the Hebrew Language* (Cambridge: Cambridge University Press, 1993), 56–62. R. Boling, *Judges,* Anchor Bible (New York: Doubleday, 1975), 101–20. A. Soggin, *Judges,* Old Testament Library (Philadelphia: Westminster Press, 1981), 80–81.

11. A. Ofer, "All the Hill Country of Judah: From a Settlement Fringe to a Prosperous Monarchy," in I. Finkelstein and N. Na'aman, eds. *From Nomadism to Monarchy: Archaeological and Historical Aspects of Early Israel* (Washington, D.C.: Biblical Archaeology Society, 1994), 110–12.

Chapter Two: Textual and Archaeological Evidence

1. 3rd ed. (Princeton: Princeton University Press, 1969), 483–90 (henceforth abbreviated ANET).

2. (Baltimore and London: Johns Hopkins University Press), 1992.

3. ANET 488–89 (EA 288 [EA is a special abbreviation, hereafter used throughout, that stands for *El Amarna* and is used for numbering the Amarna letters.]). Moran, 330–32.

4. ANET 488–89 (EA 288).

5. Moran, 147–48 (EA 77); see also 141–44 (EA 73, 74), 150–51 (EA 81), 153–54 (EA 83).

6. G. Mendenhall, *The Tenth Generation: The Origins of the Biblical Tradition* (Baltimore: Johns Hopkins University Press, 1973), 122–41. N. Gottwald, *The Tribes of Yahweh* (Maryknoll: Orbis Books, 1979), 401–9, 474–85.

7. ANET 243, 247, 254, 259. For a more complete list and discussion, see R. Giveon, *Les bédouins Shosou des documents égyptiens* (Leiden, Netherlands: E. J. Brill, 1971).

8. ANET 259.

9. (Princeton: Princeton University Press, 1992), 269–80.

10. Redford, 272–73. J. Axelsson, *The Lord Rose Up from Seir: Studies in the History and Traditions of the Negev and Southern Judah*

(Stockholm: Almquist & Wiksell, 1987), 59–61. T. Hiebert, *God of My Victory: The Ancient Hymn in Habakkuk 3*, Harvard Semitic Monographs, 38 (Atlanta: Scholars Press, 1986), 90–91. Cf. Giveon, 27–28, 74–76, 236, 241.

11. G. Ahlström, *Who Were the Israelites?* (Winona Lake, Ind.: Eisenbrauns, 1986), 59–60. T. Thompson, "The Joseph and Moses Narratives," in J. Hayes and J. M. Miller, eds., *Israelite and Judaean History* (Philadelphia: Trinity Press International, 1977), 158–59.

12. T. Dothan (New Haven and London: Yale University Press, 1982).

13. T. and M. Dothan (New York: Macmillan, 1992).

14. ANET 262–63.

15. J. Pritchard, ed., *The Ancient Near East in Pictures Relating to the Old Testament,* 2nd ed. (Princeton: Princeton University Press, 1969), 350.

16. ANET 260–62.

17. ANET 376–78. M. Lichtheim, *Ancient Egyptian Literature, vol. 2, The New Kingdom* (Berkeley: University of California Press, 1976), 73–78.

18. ANET 378.

19. M. Hasel, *"Israel* in the Merneptah Stela," *Bulletin of the American Schools of Oriental Research* 296 (1994): 45–61. See also G. Ahlström, *The History of Ancient Palestine* (Minneapolis: Fortress Press, 1993), 284–86.

20. "3,200-Year-Old Picture of Israelites Found in Egypt," *Biblical Archaeology Review* 16 (1990), no. 5:20–38.

21. "Rainey's Challenge," *Biblical Archaeology Review* 17 (1991), no. 6:56–60, 93.

22. *Ugaritic Literature* (Rome: Biblical Institute Press, 1949); *Ugaritic Textbook: Grammar, Texts in Transliteration, Cuneiform Selections, Glossary, Indices* (Rome: Biblical Institute Press, 1967).

23. *Psalms,* 3 vols., Anchor Bible (Garden City, N.Y.: Doubleday, 1966–70).

24. (Grand Rapids: Eerdmans, 1983).

25. D. N. Freedman, ed. (New York: Doubleday, 1992), vol. 6, 706–21.

26. ANET 129–55. See discussion in Hiebert, 92–93, 97–99, 102–4; and W. F. Albright, *Yahweh and the Gods of Canaan: A Histori-*

cal Analysis of Two Contrasting Faiths (Garden City, N.Y.: Doubleday, 1968), 121–22, 162.

    27. ANET 129–42.

    28. ANET 132.

    29. ANET 131.

    30. ANET 653–54.

    31. (New York: Harper & Row, 1990), 7–40.

    32. F. M. Cross and D. N. Freedman, *Studies in Ancient Yahwistic Poetry* (Missoula, Mont.: Scholars Press, 1975). See also recent commentaries on Deuteronomy, Judges and Habakkuk.

    33. M. Smith, *The Early History of God,* 15–21, 80–114.

    34. ANET 149–55.

    35. *Psalms I,* 174–80.

    36. P. Craigie, *Ugarit and the Old Testament,* 68–71.

    37. On the Assembly of the Gods, see E. T. Mullen, *The Assembly of the Gods: The Divine Council in Canaanite and Early Hebrew Literature* (Chico, Calif.: Scholars Press, 1980).

    38. (New York: Doubleday, 1990).

    39. (Seattle: University of Washington Press, 1990).

    40. (Jerusalem: Israel Exploration Society, 1988).

    41. (New Haven: Yale University Press, 1992).

    42. The evidence and lists of cities can be found in A. Mazar, *Archaeology of the Land of the Bible,* 328–34; W. Dever, *Recent Archaeological Discoveries and Biblical Research* (Seattle: University of Washington Press, 1990), 56–61; see also V. Fritz, "Conquest or Settlement: The Early Iron Age in Palestine," *Biblical Archaeologist* 50 (1987): 84–100. For an interpretation that does support a military conquest, see Y. Yadin, "Is the Biblical Account of the Israelite Conquest of Canaan Historically Reliable?" *Biblical Archaeology Review* 8 (1982), no. 2: 16–23.

    43. A. Mazar, *Archaeology of the Land of the Bible,* 334–40. See also W. Dever, "Archaeology and the Israelite 'Conquest,'" in D. N. Freedman, ed., *The Anchor Bible Dictionary,* vol. 3, 545–58; D. Hopkins, "Life on the Land: The Subsistence Strugglers of Early Israel," *Biblical Archaeologist* 50 (1987): 178–91.

    44. "To the Land of the Perizzites and the Giants: On the Israelite Settlement in the Hill Country of Manasseh," in *From Nomadism to Monarchy,* 59–60.

45. I. Finkelstein, "The Emergence of Israel: A Phase in the Cyclic History of Canaan in the Third and Second Millennia B.C.E.," in *From Nomadism to Monarchy*, 150–78.

46. A. Mazar, *Archaeology of the Land of the Bible*, 340–45. W. Dever, "Archaeology and the Israelite 'Conquest,'" 549–51.

47. A. Mazar, "The Iron Age I," in A. Ben-Tor, ed., *The Archaeology of Ancient Israel*, 287–89.

48. V. Fritz, "Conquest or Settlement," 96.

49. A. Mazar, *Archaeology of the Land of the Bible*, 345–48.

50. Ibid., 348.

51. W. Dever, "Archaeology and the Israelite 'Conquest,'" 545–58.

52. "Upper Galilee in the Late Bronze-Iron I Transition," in *From Nomadism to Monarchy*, 27.

53. "Tel Masos," in E. Stern, ed., *The New Encyclopedia of Archaeological Excavations in the Holy Land* (Jerusalem: Israel Exploration Society & Carta, 1993), vol. 3, 986–89. See also Z. Herzog, "The Beer-Sheba Valley: From Nomadism to Monarchy," in *From Nomadism to Monarchy*, 128–30, 133–34.

54. *Archaeology of the Land of the Bible*, 350–52. See also A. Mazar, "The Bull Site—An Iron Age I Open Cult Place," *Bulletin of the American Schools of Oriental Research* 247 (1982): 27–42.

55. "Kuntillet Ajrud," in D. N. Freedman, ed. *The Anchor Bible Dictionary*, vol. IV, 103–9; "Teman, Horvat," in *The New Encyclopedia of Archaeological Excavations in the Holy Land*, IV, 1458–64. See also D. N. Freedman, "Yahweh of Samaria and His Asherah," *Biblical Archaeologist* 50 (1987): 241–49.

56. W. Dever, "Khirbet el-Qom," in *The New Encyclopedia of Archaeological Excavations in the Holy Land*, IV, 1233–35.

57. *Asherah and the Cult of Yahweh in Israel* (Atlanta: Scholars Press, 1988).

58. A. Mazar, *Archaeology of the Land of the Bible*, 501–2. G. Barkay, "The Iron Age II–III," in *The Archaeology of Ancient Israel*, 360–62.

59. T. and M. Dothan, *People of the Sea*, 85–86, 91, 159–66.

60. Ibid., 218–19.

61. Ibid., 57–73, 92–94, 202–8; plates 4 and 17.

62. Ibid., 107–12.

63. Ibid., 113–17.

64. Ibid., 223–33.

65. Ibid., 153–57; plate 8.

66. Ibid., 200–202.

67. "A Comparison of Two Contemporaneous Lifestyles of the Late Second Millennium B.C.," *Bulletin of the American Schools of Oriental Research* 273 (1989): 37–55.

Chapter Three: Three Classic Models

1. *The Biblical Period from Abraham to Ezra: An Historical Survey* (New York: Harper & Row, 1963), 26.

2. "The Israelite Conquest in the Light of Archaeology," *Bulletin of the American Schools of Oriental Research* 74 (1939): 11–23; *The Biblical Period,* 27.

3. "The Israelite Conquest in the Light of Archaeology," 17–20; *The Biblical Period,* 28–29.

4. G. Archer, *Encyclopedia of Bible Difficulties* (Grand Rapids: Zondervan, 1982), 91.

5. A. Alt, *Essays on Old Testament History and Religion* (Garden City, N.Y.: Doubleday, 1967), especially "The God of the Fathers," 1–86, and "The Settlement of the Israelites in Palestine," 173–221.

6. *The History of Israel,* 2nd ed. (New York: Harper & Row, 1960), 53, 68.

7. Ibid., 71–72.

8. Ibid., 81.

9. "The Hebrew Conquest of Canaan," *Biblical Archaeologist* 25 (1962): 66–87.

10. Maryknoll: Orbis Books, 1979.

11. Ibid., 474–85.

12. Ibid., 430–34, 494.

13. I. Finkelstein, *The Archaeology of the Israelite Settlement* (Jerusalem: Israel Exploration Society, 1988). V. Fritz, "Conquest or Settlement? The Early Iron Age in Palestine," *Biblical Archaeologist* 50 (1987) 84–100.

Chapter Four: The Peoples of Canaan at the Beginning of Iron Age I

1. Sheffield, England: Sheffield Academic Press, 1991.
2. Ibid., 50–52.
3. Ibid., 170–72.
4. *The Tribes of Yahweh: A Sociology of the Religion of Liberated Israel, 1250–1050 B.C.E.* (Maryknoll: Orbis Books, 1979), 391–400.
5. W. Moran, ed., *The Amarna Letters* (Baltimore and London: Johns Hopkins University Press, 1992) 306–8 (EA 253, 254).
6. A. Mazar, *Archaeology of the Land of the Bible, 10,000–586 B.C.E.* (New York: Doubleday, 1990), 239–40.
7. *The Highlands of Canaan: Agricultural Life in the Early Iron Age* (Sheffield, England: JSOT Press, 1985).
8. *The History of Ancient Palestine* (Minneapolis: Fortress Press, 1993), 200.
9. *Egypt, Canaan, and Israel in Ancient Times* (Princeton: Princeton University Press, 1992) 275–80.
10. Gottwald, *The Tribes of Yahweh*, 391–94.
11. Ibid., 395–96.
12. *People of the Sea: The Search for the Philistines* (New York: Macmillan, 1992), 215–18.
13. Ibid., 216.
14. "Upper Galilee in the Late Bronze-Iron I Transition," in I. Finkelstein and N. Na'aman, eds., *From Nomadism to Monarchy: Archaeological and Historical Aspects of Early Israel* (Jerusalem: Yad Izhak Ben-Zvi and Israel Exploration Society, 1994), 27, 30–31.

Chapter Five: Migration and Infiltration

1. (Princeton: Princeton University Press, 1992).
2. Ibid., 257–69. See also D. Redford, *A Study of the Biblical Story of Joseph* (Leiden: E. J. Brill, 1970).
3. *Egypt, Canaan, and Israel*, 275–79.
4. Ibid., 275.
5. Ibid., 279–80.
6. Ibid., 272–73.

7. Ibid., 280.
8. Ibid., 275–76.
9. W. Dever, "How to Tell a Canaanite from an Israelite," in H. Shanks, ed., *The Rise of Ancient Israel* (Washington, D.C.: Biblical Archaeology Society, 1992), 54. G. Ahlström, *The History of Ancient Palestine* (Minneapolis: Fortress Press, 1993) 334–70.
10. *The Emergence of Israel in Canaan* (Chico, Calif.: Scholars Press, 1983). "Settlement of Canaan," in D. N. Freedman, ed., *The Anchor Bible Dictionary* (New York: Doubleday, 1992), vol. 5, 1132–35.
11. *The Emergence of Israel in Canaan*, 88.
12. "Settlement of Canaan," 1132–35.
13. Ibid., 1138.
14. Ibid., 1139.
15. *The Emergence of Israel in Canaan,* 90–91. "The Exodus from Egypt: Myth or Reality?" in H. Shanks, ed., *The Rise of Ancient Israel* (Washington, D.C.: Biblical Archaeology Society, 1992), 102–6.
16. *The Emergence of Israel in Canaan*, 91–93.
17. "Settlement of Canaan," 1141.

Chapter Six: Symbiosis

1. "Conquest or Settlement? The Early Iron Age in Palestine," *Biblical Archaeologist* 50 (1987): 84–100.
2. Ibid., 86–92.
3. Ibid., 92–96.
4. Ibid., 97. See also I. Finkelstein, *Izbet Sartah* (Oxford: Oxford University Press, 1986), 186–97.
5. Ibid., 97–98.
6. Ibid., 99.
7. "A Comparison of Two Contemporaneous Lifestyles of the Late Second Millennium B.C.," *Bulletin of the American Schools of Oriental Research* 273 (1989): 37–55.
8. (Jerusalem: Israel Exploration Society, 1988).
9. Ibid., 254–59.
10. "Ethnicity and Origin of the Iron I Settlers in the Highlands of

Canaan: Can the Real Israel Stand Up?" *Biblical Archaeologist* 59 (1996): 201.

11. *Archaeology of the Israelite Settlement,* 283–85.

12. "Ethnicity and Origin of the Iron I Settlers," 202.

13. Ibid., 206.

14. "The Emergence of Israel: A Phase in the Cyclic History of Canaan in the Third and Second Millennia B.C.E.," in I. Finkelstein and N. Na'aman, eds., *From Nomadism to Monarchy: Archaeological and Historical Aspects of Early Israel* (Jerusalem: Yad Izhak Ben-Zvi and Israel Exploration Society, 1994), 150–78.

15. *Archaeology of the Israelite Settlement,* 336–38.

16. Ibid., 348–51.

17. "Ethnicity and Origin of the Iron I Settlers," 209.

18. Ibid., 198–200.

19. Ibid., 203–4.

Chapter Seven: The First Israelites Were Canaanites

1. *Recent Archaeological Discoveries and Biblical Research* (Seattle: University of Washington Press, 1990), 56–61.

2. Ibid., 61–79.

3. Ibid., 79.

4. "How to Tell a Canaanite from an Israelite," in *The Rise of Ancient Israel,* 30.

5. Ibid., 30.

6. Ibid., 54.

7. "Ceramics, Ethnicity, and the Question of Israel's Origins," *Biblical Archaeologist* 58 (1995): 201.

8. Ibid., 209–10.

9. (Leiden, Netherlands: E. J. Brill, 1985).

10. (Sheffield, England: Sheffield Academic Press, 1990).

11. Ibid., 78–80.

12. "Israel, History of (Premonarchic Period)," in D. N. Freedman, ed., *The Anchor Bible Dictionary* (New York: Doubleday, 1992), vol. 3, 537.

13. *Ancient Israel,* 82–90.

14. "Israel, History of (Premonarchic Period)," *Anchor Bible Dictionary*, vol. 3, 537–38.

15. Ibid., 538.

16. *Ancient Israel*, 19.

17. "Israel, History of (Premonarchic Period)," *Anchor Bible Dictionary*, vol. 3, 538.

18. *The Canaanites and Their Land: The Tradition of the Canaanites* (Sheffield, England: Sheffield Academic Press, 1991), 170–72.

19. (Winona Lake, Ind.: Eisenbrauns, 1986).

20. (Minneapolis: Fortress Press, 1993).

21. Ibid., 285.

22. Ibid., 286.

23. Ibid., 337–40.

24. Ibid., 349–50.

25. (Atlanta: Scholars Press, 1993).

26. (Philadelphia: Fortress Press, 1985).

27. "Sociology (Ancient Israel)," *Anchor Bible Dictionary*, vol. 6, 83.

28. *The Hebrew Bible: A Socio-Literary Introduction,* 273–74.

29. "How My Mind Has Changed or Remained the Same," in *The Hebrew Bible in Its Social World and Ours,* xxv–xxviii.

30. "Sociology (Ancient Israel)," *Anchor Bible Dictionary*, vol. 6, 83. "Response to William Dever," in H. Shanks, ed., *The Rise of Ancient Israel* (Washington, D.C.: Biblical Archaeology Society, 1992), 71. "Historical Material Models of the Origins of Israel in the Light of Recent Palestinian Archaeology," in *The Hebrew Bible in Its Social World and Ours,* 66–67.

31. "Sociology (Ancient Israel)," *Anchor Bible Dictionary*, vol. 6, 83.

32. "Response to William Dever," 73.

33. (Sheffield, England: JSOT Press, 1987).

34. (Minneapolis: Fortress Press, 1990).

35. Ibid., 75–86.

36. Ibid., 74–87.

37. Ibid., 88.

38. Ibid., 88–92.

39. Ibid., 91–92.

Chapter Eight: Conclusions

1. See J. Flanagan, *David's Social Drama: A Hologram of Israel's Early Age* (Sheffield, England: Sheffield Academic Press, 1989); and V. Fritz and P. Davies, eds., *The Origin of the Ancient Israelite States* (Sheffield, England: Sheffield Academic Press, 1996).

2. J. Axelsson, *The Lord Rose Up from Seir: Studies in the History and Traditions of the Negev and Southern Judah* (Stockholm: Almquist & Wiksell, 1987), 59–61. D. Redford, *Egypt, Canaan, and Israel in Ancient Times* (Princeton: Princeton University Press, 1992), 372–73.

3. G. Ahlström, *Who Were the Israelites?* (Winona Lake, Ind.: Eisenbrauns, 1986), 59–60. T. Thompson, "The Joseph and Moses Narratives," in J. Hayes and J. M. Miller, eds. *Israelite and Judaean History* (Philadelphia: Westminster Press, 1977), 158–59.

4. "The Beer-Sheba Valley: From Nomadism to Monarchy," in I. Finkelstein and N. Na'aman, eds. *From Nomadism to Monarchy: Archaeological and Historical Aspects of Early Israel* (Washington, D.C.: Biblical Archaeology Society, 1994), 122–49.

Annotated Bibliography

Chapter One: The Issue

• *General introductions to the issue of the origin of the Israelites can be found in most Bible reference books. Some of the best recent ones include:*

R. Brown, J. Fitzmyer and R. Murphy, eds. *The New Jerome Biblical Commentary*. Englewood Cliffs, N.J.: Prentice-Hall, 1990. Articles on every book of the Bible and other topics, including "A History of Israel," by Addison Wright, Roland Murphy and Joseph Fitzmyer, 1219–52. Brief bibliographies are included with each article.

D. N. Freedman, ed. *The Anchor Bible Dictionary*. 6 vols. New York: Doubleday, 1992. See especially the articles "Israel, History of (Premonarchic Period)," by Niels Peter Lemche, vol. 3, 526–45; "Israel, History of (Archaeology and the Israelite 'Conquest')," by William Dever, vol. 3, 545–58; and "Settlement of Canaan," by Baruch Halpern, vol. 5, 1120–43. The articles in *The Anchor Bible Dictionary* include thorough bibliographies.

B. Metzger and M. Coogan, eds. *The Oxford Companion to the Bible*. New York: Oxford University Press, 1993. Articles on every book of the Bible and on how the Bible has been used and interpreted through the centuries.

• *Also useful in beginning to study the issue are commentaries on the biblical books that have to do with Israelite origins. The following are some of the more useful ones.*

Boling, Robert, and G. E. Wright. *Joshua* (Anchor Bible). New York: Doubleday, 1982.

Boling, Robert. *Judges* (Anchor Bible). Garden City, N.Y.: Doubleday, 1975.

Butler, Trent. *Joshua* (Word Biblical Commentary). Waco: Word Books, 1983.

Childs, Brevard. *The Book of Exodus* (Old Testament Library). Louisville: Westminster Press, 1974.

Leslie Hoppe. *Joshua, Judges, With an Excursus on Charismatic Leadership in Israel* (Old Testament Message). Wilmington: Michael Glazier, 1982. The Old Testament Message series is less technical than the others.

Alberto Soggin. *Joshua* (Old Testament Library). Philadelphia: Westminster Press, 1972.

————. *Judges* (Old Testament Library). Philadelphia: Westminster Press, 1981.

Chapter Two: Textual and Archaeological Evidence

• *A very useful collection of texts is* Ancient Near Eastern Texts Relating to the Old Testament, *James Pritchard, ed. 3rd ed. Princeton: Princeton University Press, 1969.*
(Abbreviated: ANET.)

• *More complete collections and discussions of particular texts include the following:*

Caquot, A., M. Sznycer, and A. Herdner, eds. *Textes ougaritiques: introduction, traduction, commentaire.* Vol. 1, *Mythes et légendes.* Paris: Éditions du Cerf, 1974.

Giveon, R. *Les bédouins Shosou des documents égyptiens.* Leiden, Netherlands: E. J. Brill, 1971.

Lichtheim, Miriam. *Ancient Egyptian Literature.* 3 vols. Berkeley: University of California Press, 1973–80. Most relevant for the period of the origin of the Israelites is *vol. 2, The New Kingdom.*

Moran, William, ed. *The Amarna Letters.* Baltimore and London: Johns Hopkins University Press, 1992.

• *On the archaeological background, some of the best recent general works are:*

Ben-Tor, A., ed. *The Archaeology of Ancient Israel.* New Haven: Yale University Press, 1992. Arranged by time periods; written by several leading archaeologists.

Finkelstein, I., and N. Na'aman, eds. *From Nomadism to Monarchy: Archaeological and Historical Aspects of Early Israel.* Jerusalem: Yad Izhak Ben-Zvi and Israel Exploration Society, 1994. Chapters on each region of Palestine, plus general articles on the emergence of Israel and related topics.

Mazar, Amihai. *Archaeology of the Land of the Bible, 10,000–586 B.C.E.* New York: Doubleday, 1990. Perhaps the most useful for the nonarchaeologist; well organized and clearly written.

Meyers, Eric, ed. *The Oxford Encyclopedia of Archaeology in the Near East.* 5 vols. Oxford and New York: Oxford University Press, 1997. Articles dealing with recent archaeology of the Near East; also includes material on early archaeological work and influential archaeologists.

Stern, E., ed. *The New Encyclopedia of Archaeological Excavations in the Holy Land.* Jerusalem: Israel Exploration Society and Carta, 1993. 4 vols., with articles on sites, regions and types of structures (e.g., synagogues); plenty of photos.

• *On the relationship between archaeology and biblical studies, see Leslie Hoppe,* What Are They Saying about Biblical Archaeology? *Mahwah, N.J.: Paulist Press, 1984.*

• *On the Philistines and other Sea Peoples, the best treatment is* People of the Sea: The Search for the Philistines, *by Trude and Moshe Dothan, New York: Macmillan, 1992.*

• *Periodicals aimed at the nonspecialist include* Near Eastern Archaeology *(known as* Biblical Archaeologist *before 1998) and* Biblical Archaeology Review; *the latter tends to sensationalize issues. More technical articles on archaeology can be found in* Bulletin of the American Schools of Oriental Research, Israel Exploration Journal, Journal of Near Eastern Studies and Tel Aviv.

• *On-line resources are increasing rapidly; the following are excellent, and contain links to other sites.*

The Electronically Linked Academy (TELA):
http://scholar.cc.emory.edu
Web site of Scholars Press and several of its sponsoring societies, including the Society of Biblical Literature and the American Schools of Oriental Research; one of the most useful gateways to other scholarly sites on religion and biblical studies.

The Oriental Institute—The University of Chicago:
http://www.oi.uchicago.edu/OI
Archaeological and historical information from the Oriental Institute, plus lists of other resources available on the web, including map collections, museum sites and on-line publications on the Bible.

Sacred Scripture Resources:
http://www.vocations.org/library/linkss.htm
A categorized list of resources available on the web for all areas of biblical studies; maintained by the University of St. Mary of the Lake.

Abercrombie, John, "The Archaeology of Egypt and Canaan in Ancient Times":
http://staff.feldberg.brandeis.edu/~jacka/ANEP/ANEP.html
Developed for a course at Brandeis, it is also accessible to the public. Includes texts, images, "walk-throughs" of structures as well as bibliographies.

Lloyd, Jeff, "The Edinburgh Ras Shamra Project":
http://www.ed.ac.uk/~ugarit/home.html
Contains texts and other information on the Ugaritic literature, bibliographies and links to other sites.

McDermott, John, "Israelite Origins":
http://www.loras.edu/~REL/mcdermot/origins.htm
This is the author's web site, which covers the same material as this book and will be regularly updated.

Chapter Three: Three Classic Models

• *Works by the scholars who developed the three classic models include the following:*

Conquest

Albright, W. F. "The Israelite Conquest in the Light of Archaeology." *Bulletin of the American Schools of Oriental Research* 74 (1939): 11–23.

_____. *The Biblical Period from Abraham to Ezra: An Historical Survey.* New York: Harper & Row, 1963.

_____. *Yahweh and the Gods of Canaan: A Historical Analysis of Two Contrasting Faiths.* London: Athlon Press, 1968.

Peaceful Infiltration

Alt, Albrecht. *Essays on Old Testament History and Religion.* Oxford: Blackwell, 1966.

Noth, Martin. *The History of Israel.* 2nd ed. New York: Harper & Row, 1960.

Social Revolution

Gottwald, Norman. *The Tribes of Yahweh: A Sociology of the Religion of Liberated Israel, 1250–1050 B.C.E.* Maryknoll: Orbis Books, 1979.

Mendenhall, George. "The Hebrew Conquest of Canaan." *Biblical Archaeologist* 25 (1962): 66–87.

_____. *The Tenth Generation: The Origins of the Biblical Tradition.* Baltimore: Johns Hopkins University Press, 1973.

Chapter Four: The Peoples of Canaan at the Beginning of Iron Age I

Dothan, Trude, and Moshe Dothan. *People of the Sea: The Search for the Philistines.* New York: Macmillan, 1992. Mostly on the Philistines, but also brings in the broader context of the other Sea Peoples, including a discussion on the tribe of Dan possibly coming from Sea Peoples.

Gottwald, Norman. *The Tribes of Yahweh: A Sociology of the Religion of Liberated Israel, 1250–1050 B.C.E.* Maryknoll: Orbis Books, 1979. As background for his model Gottwald includes an extensive discussion of the political and economic situations in Canaan in the Late Bronze Age and Iron Age I.

Hopkins, David. *The Highlands of Canaan: Agricultural Life in the Early Iron Age.* Sheffield, England: JSOT Press, 1985. A study of agricultural practices; useful background for analyses of Canaanite and Israelite demographics.

Lemche, Niels Peter. *The Canaanites and Their Land: The Tradition of the Canaanites.* Sheffield, England: JSOT Press, 1991. Studies what the word *Canaan* meant to ancient people, including how different parts of the Bible use the word.

Chapter Five: Migration and Infiltration

• *This and the listings for the next two chapters are not complete bibliogra-*

phies of all of these scholars' works but list only those English works most concerned with the origin of the Israelites.

Baruch Halpern

The Emergence of Israel in Canaan. Chico, Calif.: Scholars Press, 1983.

"Settlement of Canaan," in D. N. Freedman, ed., *The Anchor Bible Dictionary.* Vol. 5, 1120–43. New York: Doubleday, 1992.

"The Exodus from Egypt: Myth or Reality?" in H. Shanks, ed. *The Rise of Ancient Israel.* Washington, D.C.: Biblical Archaeology Society, 1992: 87–113.

Donald Redford

A Study of the Biblical Story of Joseph. Leiden, Netherlands: E. J. Brill, 1970.

Egypt, Canaan, and Israel in Ancient Times. Princeton: Princeton University Press, 1992.

Chapter Six: Symbiosis

Israel Finkelstein

The Archaeology of the Israelite Settlement. Jerusalem: Israel Exploration Society, 1988.

"The Emergence of Israel: A Phase in the Cyclic History of Canaan in the Third and Second Millennia B.C.E.," in I. Finkelstein and N. Na'aman, eds. *From Nomadism to Monarchy: Archaeological and Historical Aspects of Early Israel.* Jerusalem: Yad Izhak Ben-Zvi and Israel Exploration Society, 1994: 150–78.

Living on the Fringe: The Archaeology and History of the Negev, Sinai, and Neighbouring Regions in the Bronze and Iron Ages. Sheffield, England: Sheffield Academic Press, 1995.

"Ethnicity and Origin of the Iron I Settlers in the Highlands of Canaan: Can the Real Israel Stand Up?" *Biblical Archaeologist* 59 (1996): 198–212.

Volkmar Fritz

"The Israelite 'Conquest' in Light of Recent Excavations at Khirbet el-Mishnah," *Bulletin of the American Schools of Oriental Research* 241 (1981): 61–73.

"Conquest or Settlement? The Early Iron Age in Palestine," *Biblical Archaeologist* 50 (1987): 84–100.

The City in Ancient Israel. Sheffield, England: Sheffield Academic Press, 1995. Includes a chapter on the origin of the Israelites.

Chapter Seven: The First Israelites Were Canaanites

William Dever

"Asherah, Consort of Yahweh? New Evidence from Kuntillet 'Ajrud," *Bulletin of the American Schools of Oriental Research* 255 (1984): 21–37.

Recent Archaeological Discoveries and Biblical Research. Seattle: University of Washington Press, 1990.

"Archaeological Data on the Israelite Settlement: A Review of Two Recent Works," *Bulletin of the American Schools of Oriental Research* 284 (1991): 77–90.

"How to Tell a Canaanite From an Israelite," in H. Shanks, ed., *The Rise of Ancient Israel.* Washington, D.C.: Biblical Archaeology Society, 1992: 26–56.

"Israel, History of (Archaeology and the Israelite 'Conquest')," in D. N. Freedman, ed., *The Anchor Bible Dictionary.* Vol. 3, 545–58. New York: Doubleday, 1992.

"Ceramics, Ethnicity, and the Question of Israel's Origins," *Biblical Archaeologist* 58 (1995): 200–13.

Niels Peter Lemche

Early Israel: Anthropological and Historical Studies on the Israelite Society before the Monarchy. Leiden, Netherlands: E. J. Brill, 1985.

Ancient Israel: A New History of Israelite Society. Sheffield, England: JSOT Press, 1988.

"Israel, History of (Premonarchic Period)," in D. N. Freedman, ed., *The Anchor Bible Dictionary.* Vol. 3, 526–45. New York: Doubleday, 1992.

Gösta Ahlström

Who Were the Israelites? Winona Lake, Ind.: Eisenbrauns, 1986.

The History of Ancient Palestine. Minneapolis: Fortress Press, 1993.

Norman Gottwald

The Hebrew Bible: A Socio-Literary Introduction. Philadelphia: Fortress Press, 1985.

"Response to William Dever," in H. Shanks, ed., *The Rise of Ancient Israel.* Washington, D.C.: Biblical Archaeology Society, 1992: 70–75.

"Sociology (Ancient Israel)," in D. N. Freedman, ed., *The Anchor Bible Dictionary.* Vol.6, 79-80. New York: Doubleday, 1992.

The Hebrew Bible in Its Social World and Ours. Atlanta: Scholars Press, 1993. A collection of essays; most useful are "Historical Material Models of the Origins of Israel in the Light of Recent Palestinian Archaeology" and "Two Models of the Origins of Ancient Israel: Social Revolution or Frontier Development."

Robert Coote

Early Israel: A New Horizon. Minneapolis: Fortress Press, 1990.

Robert Coote and K. Whitelam. *The Emergence of Early Israel in Historical Perspective.* Sheffield, England: JSOT Press, 1987.

Other Books in This Series

What are they saying about the Prophets?
by David P. Reid, SS. CC.
What are they saying about Moral Norms?
by Richard M. Gula, S.S.
What are they saying about Sexual Morality?
by James P. Hanigan
What are they saying about Dogma?
by William E. Reiser, S.J.
What are they saying about Peace and War?
by Thomas A. Shannon
What are they saying about Papal Primacy?
by J. Michael Miller, C.S.B.
What are they saying about Matthew?
by Donald Senior, C.P.
What are they saying about Matthew's Sermon on the Mount?
by Warren Carter
What are they saying about Biblical Archaeology?
by Leslie J. Hoppe. O.F.M.
What are they saying about Theological Method?
by J.J. Mueller, S.J.
What are they saying about Virtue?
by Anthony J. Tambasco
What are they saying about Genetic Engineering?
by Thomas A. Shannon
What are they saying about Salvation?
by Rev. Denis Edwards
What are they saying about Mark?
by Frank J. Matera
What are they saying about Luke?
by Mark Allan Powell
What are they saying about John?
by Gerard S. Sloyan
What are they saying about Acts?
by Mark Allan Powell

Other Books in This Series